Happy Kids Don't Punch You in the Face

For Valerie, Avery, Holland, Scarlett, and Eden

Happy Kids Don't Punch You in the Face

A Guide to Eliminating Aggressive Behavior in School

Ben Springer, PhD, NCSP

CORWIN
A SAGE Publishing Company

Visit the companion website at
resources.corwin.com/happykids for
downloadable resources.

Happy Kids Don't Punch You in the Face

A Guide to Eliminating Aggressive Behavior in School

Ben Springer, PhD, NCSP

CORWIN

A SAGE Publishing Company

CORWIN
A SAGE Publishing Company

FOR INFORMATION:

Corwin

A SAGE Company

2455 Teller Road

Thousand Oaks, California 91320

(800) 233-9936

www.corwin.com

SAGE Publications Ltd.

1 Oliver's Yard

55 City Road

London EC1Y 1SP

United Kingdom

SAGE Publications India Pvt. Ltd.

B 1/I 1 Mohan Cooperative Industrial Area

Mathura Road, New Delhi 110 044

India

SAGE Publications Asia-Pacific Pte. Ltd.

3 Church Street

#10-04 Samsung Hub

Singapore 049483

Program Director: Jessica Allan

Associate Editor: Lucas Schleicher

Editorial Assistant: Mia Rodriguez

Production Editor: Tori Mirsadjadi

Copy Editor: Megan Granger

Typesetter: C&M Digitals (P) Ltd.

Proofreader: Eleni-Maria Georgiou

Indexer: May Hasso

Cover Designer: Candice Harman

Marketing Manager: Charline Maher

Printed in the United States of America.

ISBN: 978-1-5063-9279-0

This book is printed on acid-free paper.

18 19 20 21 22 10 9 8 7 6 5 4 3 2 1

Contents

Visit the companion website at
resources.corwin.com/happykids for
downloadable resources.

Preface

ORIGINS

Early on, there were a few years when I attributed my success with kids to "intangibles" or some sort of "knack." Fortunately, working with difficult kids has a way of knocking some sense into you (bad pun totally intended)! As much as I would have liked to believe I was endowed with "a gift" for helping kids stop punching people in the face—this was not the case. I have no delusion now that my ability to help kids decrease their aggression and increase their joy comes from anywhere but real, methodical, reproducible steps. Over the past decade, I have shared these steps with educators and parents through hundreds of training seminars, workshops, and in-services. The response to these endeavors has been overwhelmingly positive and has culminated in a comprehensive training procedure for which this book serves as source material. If anything, I have been successful in threading the needle of the pioneering work of Gerald Patterson, George Sugai, Robert Horner, Martin Seligman, Mihaly Csikszentmihalyi, and V. Mark Durand in an accessible way for educators. I could not imagine any book, approach, or strategy involving the well-being of children that didn't acknowledge the monuments of thought mentioned here.

Reading their work has not only shaped my own understanding of how to help children, but it has shaped my life as a teacher, father, psychologist, administrator, brother, son, husband, and so on. I am not a talented enough writer to detail the breadth and scope of their work here, but I feel quite comfortable providing you with their respective "scholarly highlight reels":

- Gerald Patterson has essentially explained and identified the why and how of kids' transforming into terrifying fire-breathing tyrants hell-bent on getting their way—and how to stop it from happening again! Patterson forged this theory at a critical time when several theories in the field existed, but none with a solid empirical base. It is safe to say that studying aggression in children and trying to make the world a better place was his life's work. I believe he succeeded on both counts.
- I have never felt comfortable referencing Sugai without Horner. It just seems like they go better together. (At one point in their

respective and impressive careers, they were even codirectors for the Center on Positive Behavioral Interventions and Supports at the University of Oregon.) In 2015, this dynamic duo provided an extensive retrospective on the societal impact of positive behavior supports and shared "lessons learned" in their adventures: (1) Emphasize core features and evidence-based strategies, (2) implement "systems" that support and sustain effective practices, (3) collect and use data for decision making, and (4) respect the implementation and adoption as a process. On that note, I consider the contributions of Sugai and Horner to be kind of like an Oreo cookie (made of separate but delicious parts) and school systems to be a glass of milk. When you dunk their school-wide positive behavior supports into schools, the result is pure bliss.

- Speaking of pure bliss, we can thank Martin Seligman for actually understanding how important bliss is to mental health. Seligman has been credited for articulating and expanding the field of Positive Psychology in the new millennium. His work has shifted the emphasis of mental health from what is broken to what is actually working. In 2002 he wrote, "Positive Psychology takes you through the countryside of pleasure and gratification, up into the high country of strength and virtue, and finally to the peaks of lasting fulfillment: meaning and purpose."

- Fun fact about Mihaly Csikszentmihalyi: You pronounce his name "chick-sent-me-high." Another fun fact: His work has resulted in what must be the most specific, concrete path to happiness the world has ever known. In other words, before Csikszentmihalyi's work, happiness was thought to be a secret path known only to few. Now there's a paved highway, and he's provided the street signs.

- Delving into the power of optimism in our roles as parents, educators, and school-based practitioners has led V. Mark Durand to some astounding findings: Attitude, it seems, really is everything. This is not some new-age mind-over-matter gimmick. Durand has found through rigorous research that our level of optimism may be the deciding factor in whether or not our behavioral strategies succeed or fail.

Finally, while I plan to infuse the work of the aforementioned authors and researchers, I will also be including detailed episodes and stories from my time spent working directly with children. I consider these episodes quasi-sacred. Many of these episodes have been the most rewarding of my life. Some of these episodes have been downright awful. I will obviously not be sharing any personal or identifiable information, but please note that these episodes have indeed taken place. My intent for sharing them is the direct result of feedback on hundreds of evaluations from trainings I have conducted. Clearly, the real-life stories of children, their teachers, and their parents resonate with people. There are many reasons why I believe this to be the case, and I will touch on them throughout the book. For now, suffice it to state that the stories, at the very least, are memorable. I believe that stories are what actually stay with people—not the facts. So I have decided to explicitly use the tools of authentic narratives from my practice to help the reader conceptualize the facts. What are these facts? Consistency trumps randomness, love trumps aggression, and kids thrive on meaningful relationships—just like the rest of us.

Overview: What This Book Will Do for You

Happy Kids Don't Punch You in the Face exists to bridge the principles most practitioners have been exposed to for the past few decades (e.g., Response to Intervention/Multi-Tiered Systems of Support, Applied Behavior Analysis) and integrate them into the best practices of Positive Psychology (e.g., happiness, flow, optimism training). Modern-day practitioners and educators deserve to know more about behavior management and discipline procedures through the lens of Positive Psychology (an approach emphasizing the importance of relationships and humanism). In the field of education, these shifts in approaches can often be referred to as inevitable "pendulum swings" or "one more thing on the plate" that educators begrudgingly tolerate. It will be refreshing to note that *Happy Kids* is not part of a trendy pendulum swing, nor is it anything extra on the plate; it *is* the plate. The approaches in *Happy Kids* present a comprehensive method of how we should be interacting with children, particularly children exhibiting aggressive and disruptive behavior.

We simply know too much about what works to pretend that any new approach will be around the corner. We have reached the corner and seen the horizon. *Happy Kids* is a summary of these approaches, old, new, modern—and all of the above. First readers will review why aggression exists and manifests so early in childhood. Then readers will say good-bye to approaches that simply do not work. Readers will also pay homage to the ubiquitous "triangle of prevention," as well as the principles of Applied Behavior Analysis. Finally, readers will (re)discover the significance of happiness, relationships, and optimism in everything they do.

RATIONALE

The rationale behind *Happy Kids Don't Punch You in the Face* is to help practitioners successfully reduce the frequency and intensity of aggressive behavior by infusing the best practices of Positive Psychology into preventive systems (e.g., Multi-Tiered Systems of Support) and classic behavior management approaches (e.g., Applied Behavior Analysis). Back in 1997, Mash and Terdal indicated that the goal of any successful behavioral treatment must (a) be clearly defined, (b) have relevance to the presenting complaints of the stakeholders, (c) have significance for the child's present and future adjustment, and (d) be grounded in an adequate theory of how and why the behavior developed and maintained.

Many texts and approaches include the structure identified by Mash and Terdal. Where *Happy Kids* differs is the level and depth of attention paid to the child's future adjustment. The plans and strategies provided for children exhibiting aggressive behavior will certainly address how to help "in the moment" but not at the sacrifice of the future. Each plan presented in *Happy Kids* is built with an eye on the child's well-being and relationships beyond their time in the school setting. With that in mind, *Happy Kids Don't Punch You in the Face* will

- serve as a desk reference for current research, theory, and practice in the areas of Multi-Tiered Systems of Support, Applied Behavior Analysis, and Positive Psychology;
- provide ready-to-use strategies and tools to help students succeed and be happy in school, at home, and in life;
- be different from every other book on the topic, because it is fresh, fun, and organized for modern-day (see also: crazy-busy) educators, administrators, counselors, and therapists; and
- provide a unique reading experience where formal theories and constructs of human behavior are braided with an informal, conversational tone.

GOALS

As much as I want this book to be the catalyst for fundamental changes in the way we treat and support children in school, I really just want it to help readers in the following ways:

1. Identify the roots of aggression in children

2. Learn effective strategies to prevent aggression in children

3. Respond safely to a child's aggression

4. Build compassionate relationships with children

5. Adapt to the modern-day circumstances of children in school

To do so, this book contains my best effort to organize the particular set of methodologies I have enlisted over the past 20 years to help kids struggling with aggressive behaviors. These methodologies or procedures have a significant amount of research supporting their efficacy (DuPaul & Stoner, 1994; Durand, 2011, 2015; Jenson, Olympia, Farley, & Clark, 2004; Patterson, 1982; Patterson, Dishion, & Chamberlain, 1993; Sailor, Dunlap, Sugai, & Horner, 2009; Suldo & Shaffer, 2008).

Certainly, I have infused some of my own personality and understanding with these procedures—not because they need any refinement, just some freshening up. Some may argue, "If it's not broke, why fix it?" I'm not aiming to fix anything; it's just that those of us working in modern-day school systems can smell it. We know almost immediately if a behavior management approach has become stale. Despite the value of tried-and-true strategies found in the research literature, it seems as though behavior management requires a constant reshuffling and refreshing. Not because we're fickle and impatient, but because it has always been this way. It turns out that effective behavior management has always been dependent on the oft-forgotten variable of social validity (aka consumer satisfaction). Basically, modern-day educators are also modern-day consumers. If a behavior management system doesn't meet their consumer-based standards, it becomes stale or even extinct (Wolf, 1978). *Happy Kids* is fresh because it has to be. Practitioners are busy and want the current research literature and tools right now. There's nothing wrong with that. *Happy Kids* isn't going to beat practitioners over the head with heavy-handed peer-reviewed-journal jargon. *Happy Kids* has taken current best practices and arranged them so you can do your job with confidence.

INTENDED AUDIENCE

This book is intended for a broad range of practitioners and personnel working with school-age children. The content has been previously provided (via training seminars) to hundreds of educators with backgrounds in general education, special education, school psychology, school counseling, administration, and pupil transportation. The content is also valuable for classified employees such as paraprofessionals and bus attendants. In fact, one of the driving philosophies of *Happy Kids* is that there is an important role for everyone working with a student exhibiting aggressive or dangerous behavior. Really, this book is intended to help anyone interested in (a) the reasons why children become aggressive, (b) effective methods in preventing aggressive behavior, and (c) explicit steps to respond to aggressive behavior.

ANTICIPATED USES

Happy Kids Don't Punch You in the Face is anticipated to help busy practitioners, always up against the clock, with some ready-to-use strategies and easily accessible content regarding best practices in managing student aggression. In other words, *Happy Kids* is designed to be in the reader's hands as opposed to on the reader's bookshelf. Practitioners can feel comfortable carrying this book with them to study and reference as they work with students and their school teams. An individual practitioner (e.g., teacher, counselor, psychologist, administrator) may use this book to gain a deeper understanding of best practices, as well as to gain immediate access to tools. This book may also serve as the topic of a book study for teams to work through as they are presented with challenging student behavior. It is important to me that the content, strategies, and tools within *Happy Kids* be shared liberally. As educators, our collective efficacy is dependent on each of us sharing what we know. In addition to an easily accessible handbook, *Happy Kids* is also anticipated to be the source material for comprehensive trainings for school personnel working with children exhibiting aggressive and/or dangerous behavior. Training seminars are available for any practitioners eager to apply the principles in *Happy Kids* to their schools and/or districts.

THE ORGANIZATION OF *HAPPY KIDS DON'T PUNCH YOU IN THE FACE*

With the exception of the introductory section and the concluding sections, *Happy Kids* is divided into seven core chapters. Each of the chapters is organized into two parts: the content and a tools section.

The content comprises most of the chapter and is designed for your inner nerd. I tend to believe most of the concepts within *Happy Kids* are genuinely interesting and warrant some geeking out on your part. In fact, the more time you take to mine this material, the more depth you will begin to carry with you as you build your own capacity and the capacity of your teams.

The tools section describes the ready-to-use strategies related to their respective chapters and content. Some chapters may have multiple tools; some may have only a few. The goal of the tools section is to have something ready once you've covered a concept and feel like implementing some of the strategies.

In Chapter 1, we will revisit the theories of human development related to the onset of aggression. We will also be introduced to the pioneering work of Gerald Patterson in detail. We will learn about the significance of Patterson's concept of the "coercive cycle" and the way his work has provided the general consensus for how and why aggressive behavior is maintained. Finally, by reviewing Patterson's work, we will learn what components are essential in every single behavioral strategy we attempt hereafter.

In Chapter 2, we will survey the list of the archaic, ineffective (and in some cases harmful) approaches that still exist in our schools. It may be surprising how many of these approaches are still used and how many of our colleagues still support their use. After surveying what does not work, we will have built a compendium of resources and rebuttals to share with team members and thus hopefully avoid the pitfalls that so many teams sink into.

In Chapter 3, we will pay homage to the ubiquitous "triangle of prevention," but we won't stop there. In addition to the value of quality preventive systems, we will spend time on how to use the contents in this book and its trainings to help principals and administrators facilitate authentic systems of prevention in the school setting. As wonderful as the triangle of prevention is as a construct, we must acknowledge that it has begun to lose some of its luster. Why? Because it has been presented to every single educator in some form or fashion for the past 15 years, and to what end? We don't need the triangle to tell us how to do it anymore. We just need to do it. Chapter 3 will help break down the steps to make it happen.

In Chapter 4, we will reach what is essentially the heart of the entire *Happy Kids Don't Punch You in the Face* approach: real-life applications of Positive Psychology. This chapter will cover the pioneering work of Seligman and really dig deep into Csikszentmihalyi's work on flow or optimal experience. This chapter will also visit the work of Thomas Kehle and Melissa Bray and their conceptualizations of how to infuse Positive Psychology into the school setting. Chapter 4 establishes the research-based, oft-overlooked benefits of Positive Psychology and why it should start taking more of a central role in our efforts to help kids.

Chapter 5 will (re)introduce the tried-and-true principles of Applied Behavior Analysis (ABA). For those of us familiar with these approaches, ABA can get a bad rap for being overly technical, cumbersome, and robotic. Not because its principles don't work but because there is such a preciousness associated with their use. In the past few years in particular, the prevalence of Board Certified Behavior Analysts (BCBAs) has had an unintended effect in the school setting. School teachers and team members have been led to believe that only BCBAs or PhDs in psychology have the background and training to apply principles of ABA. Certainly,

BCBAs and PhDs have a specialized understanding of ABA, but the letters next to names are no precursor to understanding ABA-based principles in behavior management. Not everybody on a child's team has graduate degrees and specialized training. In other words, ABA is not just for the few; it has applications for all. The more team members who become familiar with the principles of ABA, the better. The trick is facilitating the dialogue and the access to the approaches associated with ABA—and this chapter has you covered.

Chapter 6 will provide you and your team with authentic resources about the statistically significant findings of remaining optimistic in the face of student aggression. This chapter will cover the work of V. Mark Durand and incorporate what he and his team have discovered about optimism training and its effects on improving behavioral interventions. Students exhibiting aggression are difficult to work with, pure and simple. The temptation to complain and allow the negativity of the situation to overwhelm team members is real. This chapter will prepare you and your team to acknowledge the difficulty, breathe it in, and move forward with hope.

Chapter 7 will organize all the content and tools from Chapters 1 through 6 into a comprehensive approach to helping children reduce their aggressive outbursts and increase their happiness. You may be tempted to jump right to this chapter and get started on helping a student with whom you work. While I don't recommend it, you can certainly give it a shot. I would rather you spend some time digging deeper into the concepts shared in Chapters 1 through 6. The entire philosophy of *Happy Kids Don't Punch You in the Face* is that the kids are worth the effort. Make the effort to familiarize yourself with the content of this book and you won't regret it. Just like everything in this world, the growth comes from the work. (Note: I also know you're terribly busy, so yeah, if Chapter 7 helps you right now—great!)

This book will conclude with a complete "Where Are They Now?" section dedicated to the resolution of some of the behavior plans I drafted for the students mentioned in the book. I would hate not to provide you with some closure on Trevor, Luis, Annie, Chrissie, Samantha, and Tino (some outcomes perfect, some imperfect). It is worth noting that with the exception of Tino's scenario, each of the student scenarios in this book took place in the regular school setting. The highlighted students exhibiting dangerous and aggressive behavior were all treated and supported in school districts practicing inclusion for students of all abilities. As such, the teams with whom I worked were multidisciplinary, representing practitioners from general education, special education, and administration.

SPECIAL FEATURES

Modern-day practitioners need tools, and they need them now. The special features within *Happy Kids* are not only designed to be immediately accessible; they are designed to be shared in collaboration with school teams. In each of the tools sections, there are links to beautiful PDFs and high-resolution PNG files. These digital files have been designed to be downloaded directly to your computer or smartphone for your use and to be shared over social media with colleagues and, well, the world! These PDF and PNG files contain two types of resources: infographics and templates. The infographics are colorful, high-resolution digital files summarizing key concepts found in the chapters. When done correctly, infographics are stunning visual portrayals of concepts and/or processes. The idea of a template is pretty self-explanatory. The templates within *Happy Kids* are ready to use on their own, or you can adapt them to your individual needs. For example, when covering the principles of Applied Behavior Analysis, there is a beautifully illustrated template titled "The Behavior Race." This template breaks down the formal process of a functional behavioral assessment and a solid, defendable behavior intervention plan.

Acknowledgments

I would like to acknowledge Curtis Linton (and his brother Trent) for introducing me to Jessica Allan, Meg Granger, Tori Mirsadjadi, and the rest of the team at Corwin. I would also like to acknowledge my very own gallery of support, including Valerie, Alex, Barbara, Justin, Ben, Paul, Jason, and Jim. There is no way this book sees the light of day without the wonderful people listed above.

PUBLISHER'S ACKNOWLEDGMENTS

Corwin gratefully acknowledges the contributions of the following reviewers:

Melissa Nixon
Director of Title I
Guilford County Schools
Greensboro, NC

Lena Marie Rockwood
High School Assistant Principal
Revere Public Schools
Revere, MA

Christine Grace
School Psychologist
St. Mary's County Public Schools
Leonardtown, MD

Vikki Kelly
Teacher
Carroll ISD/Carroll Middle School
Southlake, TX

Lisa Graham
Director, Special Education
Berkeley Unified School District
Berkeley, CA

Gloria Avolio
School Counselor–Instructional Mentor
Hillsborough County Public Schools
Tampa, FL

Dawn Spurlock
Statewide Special Education Instructional Coordinator, Idaho SESTA
Boise State University, Center for School Improvement and Policy
Studies
Boise, ID

Vicki McFarland
Learning Matters Educational Group
Director of Federal Programs
Glendale, AZ

Dr. Joyce Stout
School Counselor
Redondo Beach Unified School District
Torrance, CA

About the Author

Ben Springer is an award-winning Nationally Certified School Psychologist. Ben received his master's and doctoral degrees in educational psychology from the University of Utah. He studied neuropsychological assessment, counseling, school-wide positive behavior supports, bullying prevention programs, parental involvement, evidence-based practice, autism, and social skills instruction. He works as the director of special education in Wasatch County School District in Heber City, Utah.

For the past 15 years, Ben has been conducting trainings and in-services for schools, hospitals, and clinics on managing difficult student behaviors. Ben has become a popular speaker and presenter for his trainings on *Happy Kids Don't Punch You in the Face* and his keynote addresses on autism ("Autism Is a Burrito") and ADHD ("ADHD: The Goods"). Ben has presented at the University of Utah, St. Marks Hospital Rounds, Heber Valley Pediatrics, Summit Pediatrics, Utah Valley University, and the Southwest Educational Development Center.

In 2017, Ben created Totem PD, a professional development company for educators and mental health practitioners working with school-age children.

Ben is married to his middle school sweetheart (it's a thing) and has four lovely daughters. Ben enjoys a crisp Diet Coke, backpacking, fishing, and collecting comic books.

Introduction
The Lentil Incident

Mrs. Tanney had only the best intentions for these lentils. They were supposed to be part of a Pinterest-worthy Thanksgiving-themed crafting activity for her first-grade class. Her students were supposed to use the multicolored lentils to bring designs of turkeys and pilgrim hats to life. There's no way she could have predicted that her decision to bring the innocent little legumes into her classroom would result in one of the most catastrophic moments in her career. There's no way she could have predicted the lentil incident.

The lentil incident began at approximately 9:42 a.m. I arrived in Mrs. Tanney's classroom after she and her students had successfully executed a "room clear" procedure. It's a common practice for classroom teachers when a student becomes aggressive or destructive. When I got there, the other students had quietly left the room and were waiting for the situation to be resolved before they came back. It was a procedure I had helped Mrs. Tanney implement based on the behaviors of a student named Trevor. Trevor was intelligent and funny, and his floppy blond hair barely covered the steely resolve of his brown eyes. Trevor was also not a big fan of following the rules, and sometimes being told what to do aggravated his serious temper.

I had gotten to know and respect Trevor over the few weeks leading up to this moment. Not only had I performed his IQ test—incredibly high scores—but I had also conducted three or four functional behavioral assessments, all of which translated to roughly 4 hours of direct observation of his behaviors. I genuinely liked the kid, but he was also temperamental, moody, and explosive.

As I entered the room, I immediately found myself in a classic first-grade standoff. On one side of the table stood the school counselor, the principal, Mrs. Tanney, and me. On the opposite side stood Trevor. Essentially, it came down to four adults with a combined educational experience of about 100 years, and Trevor, a 7-year-old who wouldn't blink if a train was bearing down on him. On the table that separated us, I happened to notice Mrs. Tanney's five neatly organized bins of lentils.

If you were to slow down time, what happened next would have looked something like this: I made eye contact with Trevor, who met my gaze with a confident smile. I gave a firm verbal command—something like, "Trevor, you need to come with me. You need to tell me what happened." Trevor glanced at the lentils. I took the bait and glanced, too. In the split second that it took me to realize how that small reflex reinforced Trevor's impulse, I attempted to close the ground between us—but I was too late. Trevor lunged forward and grabbed two bins of lentils, one in each hand. He lifted them off the table and furiously shook them until the four of us—and our 100 years of combined experience—were caught in the middle of a lentil tsunami. In a fraction of a moment, what began as the autumnal crafting activity of Mrs. Tanney's dreams ended up as the lentil incident of our nightmares.

The day was lost and the feelings were dour. What I remember most (besides shaking the lentils out of my pants the rest of the day) was the looks of bewilderment from my colleagues. Mrs. Tanney certainly did not understand this level of disrespect, and it took something from her, I think, or it simply added a layer of disillusionment. The principal was desperate for answers and was most certainly going to be receiving calls from parents concerned about the level of disruption in the class. Unbeknownst to us at the time, the lentil incident was the final straw for the school counselor, as she pleaded with the district office for a change in assignment.

As low as that moment was for each of us, it felt like a distant memory 6 months later. In Trevor's transition meeting from first to second grade, Mrs. Tanney was his most vocal advocate and itemized every strategy, every approach she felt would work best for him and his new teacher. The principal sat smiling and joking with Trevor's parents in the same meeting. The school counselor had not been reassigned and appeared rejuvenated by Trevor's progress and the support from her school team. I sat in the meeting with my stacks of graphs, plans, notes, and assessments, pleasantly surprised by the demeanor of the team. How did we get there? How did we go from suffering a humiliating assault of lentil beans to becoming a team with a fresh sense of purpose, ready to take on the world?

As confident as I was that our assessments, plans, and data-based team decisions contributed to Trevor's improvement, there was more to it than that. I can almost guarantee that Mrs. Tanney's resolve to keep working with Trevor despite the significant amount of stress he caused her was a big component in the change. I know that the principal's support of Mrs. Tanney in this resolve was essential to that success. There were many opportunities for the principal to opt for extended school suspensions and manifest determinations, but she did not. Trevor's parental involvement undoubtedly contributed to Trevor's improvement. Additionally, the district office's response to the school counselor's concerns and reassurance of support was also significant. Certainly, each of these factors contributed to the dramatic change in behavior we witnessed in the months following the lentil incident. Yet the more interesting conclusion was *how*. How did all these moving parts (parts that—for a moment in time—appeared irrevocably broken) come together? Was it really due to all our collaboration, compassion, and hard work? I've been part of a lot of teams that were collaborative, compassionate, and worked very hard, and yet the results were not like this. Something was different. . . .

Trevor was happy.

Deep down, every educator and mental health professional knows that at the end of the day, any meaningful progress really comes down to the individual. Obviously, the environment, compassionate team members, and parents can help, but they can't do it all. If Trevor's mood and general outlook on life in first grade didn't improve, neither would his behavior. So how did Trevor "get happy"? (It wasn't medication. Trevor's parents considered him too young for an intensive regimen.)

The recipe for how Trevor found some joy and happiness is what *Happy Kids Don't Punch You in the Face* is all about. Yet this book is not just a case study on Trevor. The recipe has worked for many more students from many more walks of life. We will be hearing more about the stories of the other students and school teams that have followed this recipe. More important, much of this recipe you already know—and I know that. I will not be simply regurgitating the common tropes of behavior management (although I will be spending some time reviewing them, because, c'mon, they work pretty darn well). I will be integrating these behavioral principles into a format that expands and broadens their use into the big picture. What is the big picture? you ask. The big picture is taking on what is really important in life, school, family, and beyond:

the pursuit of happiness.

We know that happier kids are more resilient, more capable of taking on the challenges life throws at them. We know that competence in an academic area is really only one part of the happiness puzzle. There is so much more we can work toward when spending time with our youth. I know it's not unicorns and rainbows all the time, but we have got to start acknowledging that any behavior plan we create and any school team we organize must focus on broader outcomes than simply following directions and completing work assignments in school.

The recipe we followed for Trevor (and all the kids with whom I've worked) always begins with getting the team of adults on the same page about a few things. Particularly, we review the root causes of aggression, because everyone on the team inevitably asks "Why?" after getting punched in the face. Then we jettison anything we know does not work.

There is simply not enough time in the school day or in the school year to spend any on approaches that don't work. We also acknowledge that preventive systems really are as effective as advertised in the research literature. After working to accept the power in prevention, we get our feet wet in modern iterations of applied psychology. We dabble in Applied Behavior Analysis, enlisting effective tools to help change behavior as we learn to wrap our heads around a post-disorder, post-disability world where the focus is not on the deficits or excesses of behavior, but on the individual's path to happiness.

Once the team has covered these areas, we put in the work, the effort, and the refinement necessary for any approach to succeed. *Happy Kids Don't Punch You in the Face* is not a one-size-fits-all approach (and you and I both know to be wary of such claims). However, the *Happy Kids* approach lends itself nicely to the modern-day school setting, which is so dependent on collaboration. By sharing the information in this book with your colleagues, more consensus (and by default—consistency) can be applied to a behavior problem. The more consistency that can be applied to a behavior problem, the more successful the outcome will be. The more successful the outcome is, the happier the target student will be. The happier the target student is, the more lasting improvement and change can be sustained. Clearly, I'm oversimplifying this process a bit, but this is just the introduction. The rest of the book will go into detail about how we can help kids stop punching us in the face. Enjoy!

The Roots of Aggression and the Coercive Cycle

This aggression will not stand, man.

—*The Big Lebowski* (1998)

On a cold February morning, I received a panicked phone call from a preschool classroom. Mrs. LaVecki reported that Luis had been attacking his peers repeatedly and was now hiding beneath a table in the corner of the room. When I entered the room, Luis had left his hideout under the table and was screaming at a boy named Henry. Henry did not appear too frightened and was holding his ground. From what I could gather, Luis wanted Henry's Buzz Lightyear toy, and Henry was not going to give it up. Luis then began to scream louder.

As I approached Luis, out of habit I engaged in one of my dumbest moves. I call it the "crouch 'n' smile." Without thinking, I would crouch down, smile, and say something like, "Hiya, pal! How ya doin'?" Well, I performed the crouch-'n'-smile maneuver with Luis, and in a split second he scratched my face with his unusually long fingernails. Mrs. LaVecki and her paraprofessional gasped audibly. The scratches hurt (burned even), but I didn't realize the marks they had left until Mrs. LaVecki asked if I needed a paper towel. Luis had left me with three bright red stripes across my cheeks and nose. After quickly dabbing my face, I provided Luis with a seat away (a consequence wherein Luis sat in a nearby chair for a minute or two, turned away from what had set him off, e.g., the Buzz

Lightyear toy and me). Luis sat and screamed while I proceeded to help Mrs. LaVecki in the classroom. Luis eventually calmed and began participating in the class routines. I jotted down some notes and told Mrs. LaVecki that I would follow up with some strategies. (I also requested that Luis's parents attempt to trim his fingernails.)

When I got home later that day, one of my daughters asked what had happened. While at work, I had accepted the scratches on my face as my own fault, but it was slightly more embarrassing to reveal to my daughter that I had gotten worked over by a 3-year-old. (So of course I told her I was attacked by a giant vampire bat while spelunking for rare gems.)

Every morning for a week or so, when I looked in the mirror I was reminded of two things: The crouch-'n'-smile maneuver had to go, and tiny 3-year-olds can cause a lot of damage. The experience also left me thinking about what had caused Luis to become so explosive and aggressive at such a young age. I mean, he totally scratched my face without thinking twice about it. Why?

Sure, toddlers and preschoolers tend to get upset easily, and they can impulsively slap, kick, hit, and bite. Oddly enough, these sorts of behaviors can be typical for preschool-age kids. They become a problem only when they happen too frequently and begin negatively impacting family and peer relationships. When aggression becomes persistent in little kids, it is a good idea to consider immediate intervention. When kids exhibit these behaviors at an early age, they are at greater risk for developing more chronic problems throughout their life span (Bullis, Benz, Johnson, & Hollenbeck, 2000; Coie, Dodge, & Kupersmidt, 1990; Elksnin & Elksnin, 1998; Lahey & Loeber, 1994; Robinson, Smith, Miller, & Brownell, 1999). Even more troubling is that fewer than 10% of the young children showing signs of problem behaviors receive services for these difficulties (Kazdin & Kendall, 1998).

Is it any wonder that aggression and defiance are among the most frequent reasons families and schools refer children to mental health programs (Johnson, Wahl, Martin, & Johansson, 1973; Patterson, 1976, 1982; Patterson, Reid, & Dishion, 1992)? Over half of all referrals are for oppositional or aggressive behavior (Patterson, 1993).

WHAT DOES ALL THIS MEAN?

Aggression is common and difficult to manage, and parents don't have many options. When push comes to shove (bad pun totally intended), schools may be the last resort for kids and their parents. Fortunately, schools can be ideal institutions for addressing aggressive behavior in youths. Schools actually have the infrastructure to facilitate early identification, early intervention, prevention, support services, and home/community outreach

(Gresham, 2004). Understanding this dynamic is going to be essential as you work in your role to build capacity in your school. At first glance, I know schools can appear to be full of barriers rather than opportunities, yet it doesn't have to be that way. After consuming this chapter, you will be able to explain to your school team (a) why aggression exists, (b) why it persists, and (c) how to prevent it from happening.

THE ROOTS OF AGGRESSION: A TWO-WAY STREET?

An astounding amount of work has been done regarding the etiology of aggression (Cohn, 1995; Gerra et al., 1997; Jennings & Matthews, 1985; Kindlon et al., 1995; Lorber, 2004; Wolfe, Fairbank, Kelly, & Bradlyn, 1983). Most of what I have been able to find on the topic concludes with some sort of statement like this: *Analyses reveal a complex constellation of interactive effects contributing to the onset of aggression.* In other words, "It's complicated" or "It depends." While these conclusions are probably valid, they are totally unsatisfying. I reject the premise that because the development of aggression is complex we must "proceed with caution" when deciding what to do about it. Obviously, the manifestation of aggression in youth is a complex issue, but it is an issue that has been studied and explored for centuries. When we dig deep enough for the roots of aggression, we actually end up with only two (diverging) theories: nature and nurture. All roads in the nature-versus-nurture debate lead back to two men. On one side of the coin, we have John Locke (1632–1704); on the other side of the coin, we have Jean-Jacques Rousseau (1712–1778).

Side A: Tabula Rasa

In a nutshell, a long time ago, writing by candlelight, Locke proposed that the child's mind was a tabula rasa, or blank slate. As far back as 1690, Locke raised the nurture flag high when he stated, "Whence has it all the materials of reason and knowledge? To this I answer, in one word, from *experience*. In that all our knowledge is founded" (Bk. 2, Ch. 1, Sec. 2; emphasis in original). There you have it. Way before Ivan Pavlov, John B. Watson, and B. F. Skinner, Locke was writing about how environment (antecedents) and associations (operant conditioning) impact our development.

Side B: Following Nature's Inner Promptings

Rousseau's contributions to the field of child development were so profound that he is still considered the father of developmental psychology. He was one of the first people on the planet to conceptualize an inner biological timetable for development, a perspective that was far ahead of his time. He believed learning was best when educators slowed things down and gave children a chance to learn in ways that came naturally.

While Locke and Rousseau may be considered the fathers of the nature-versus-nurture debate, what does that tell us about aggression? Let's start with Team Nurture (aka the learning theorists): Locke, Watson, and Skinner.

Is Aggression Learned?

The learning theorists would answer yes. In what are perhaps the most definitive studies on the subject, Skinner demonstrated that while individuals may act freely, they are essentially controlled by the consequences of their actions. These consequences can be organized purposefully or haphazardly into schedules of reinforcement shaping the onset of aggression (or any behavior, for that matter).

There you have it; aggression is totally learned—and you knew that already. You've seen children get away with aggression on the playground, in the classroom, and at the grocery store. The reason you see this so often is because aggression tends to work. Our world has very few authentically effective consequences for aggression. Kids learn at very early ages that the fastest way to get the toy they want and a peer has is to punch that peer in the face. By the time a parent or teacher shows up, the child has already received the immediate gratification of getting their hands on the toy (even if for only a few seconds).

In addition to learning aggression through instant gratification, kids can learn to be aggressive just by proximity. In 1965, Albert Bandura introduced social learning theory and with his seminal Bobo doll study made a remarkable observation: Kids who witnessed adults pummeling a Bobo doll (an inflatable clown with a weighted base) were more likely to beat the air out of the inflatable Bobo than were kids not exposed to the aggression. In a disturbing observation, the kids with only subtle exposure to the modeled aggression even came up with new ways (ways that were not modeled) to hurt Bobo (e.g., using throwing darts and pointing a toy gun at Bobo). So can we state that aggression is learned? Yes, yes we can. Let's ask the next question.

Is Aggression Innate?

This is kind of a scary thought. Is aggression prewired? Can kids be predisposed to act aggressively? Is aggression (*gulp*) inherited? Interestingly, Team Nature's roots of Rousseau, Maria Montessori, and Jean Piaget never really examine this. We just gather from developmental theory that human beings follow their "inner promptings" and that while each individual follows a similar developmental sequence, not all individuals do so at the same rate. So we turn to modern-day theories on genetics to help define these inner promptings and where they originate. The deepest we're going to explore genetics will be in taking a look at twin studies.

What are twin studies, you ask? Twin studies are valuable tools that help us understand the differences between traits we inherit (genetics) and traits we develop because of our environment. Twin studies are helpful because they rely on the difference between monozygotic (identical) and dizygotic (fraternal) pairs of twins. Identical twins share all of each other's genes, whereas non-identical twins share only half of each other's genes. Because identical twins share the same genome, any differences between twins may be attributed to their environments, not genetics.

These studies have zeroed in on a comparison between identical and non-identical twins with respect to aggressive behavior. By doing this, the total difference of aggression can be divided into heritability, shared environmental factors, and nonshared environmental factors. Shared environmental factors refer to nongenetic influences that contribute to similarity within pairs of twins. Nonshared environmental factors are experiences that cause siblings to differ in their aggressive behavior. These comparisons control for both genetic and environmental influences and have demonstrated that aggressive traits are heritable (Tuvblad & Baker, 2011).

Although there is some variability across these types of studies, most every study has concluded that there are "significant genetic contributions to aggression in childhood" (DiLalla, 2002; Edelbrock, Rende, Plomin, & Thompson; 1995; Eley, Lichtenstein, & Stevenson, 1999).

So is aggression innate? Yes. This should come as no surprise. When we think of our family trees, rarely do we think past our great-grandpa and great-grandma. It is sobering to really consider our genetic family trees. They are incredibly vast. At the end of the day, our genetic inheritance comes down to a roll of the dice. You also already knew that. If you have children or basically know any child, you know that they come into this world with their very own traits. Sure, we see some of our familial traits in our children but not always. We know kids come to us with their own tendencies.

There you have it. Aggression has been puzzled over and studied for hundreds of years. While the nature-versus-nurture debate is an interesting one, modern-day thought and practice have left us with a nice big Jackson Pollock-esque picture of aggression in children. Aggression may be the result of the environment, genes, or (if we're really lucky) both.

SO NOW WHAT?

Fortunately, a gentleman by the name of Gerald Patterson has figured this all out for us. Essentially, Patterson has acknowledged these complexities and realized that none of them render aggression untreatable. According to Patterson, there are things we can do to minimize the effects of aggression and help kids and families move on. How did Patterson reach these wonderfully confident conclusions? Impressive scholarly acumen and brilliant research design, of course. Prepare yourselves for the work of Patterson and his colleagues from the Oregon Social Learning Center (OSLC)! Prepare yourselves for coercion theory!

THE GENERAL CONSENSUS ON AGGRESSION

Coercion theory (Patterson, 1982; Patterson et al., 1992; Reid, Patterson, & Snyder, 2002) was developed by Patterson and other scientists at OSLC, which is still operating. Essentially, Patterson and OSLC have collected hundreds of video-recorded observations of parents and children interacting in real-life settings. Through a rigorous method of coding the behaviors of both the children and their parents (same kids, same parents over multiple years, across several longitudinal designs), Patterson and his colleagues have concluded that adults and kids basically train each other to behave in ways that increase the probability that the child will develop aggression. In fact, Patterson's work has led to what is considered the general consensus on why and how aggression is manifested and maintained in childhood:

> We believe that reinforcement for aggression is provided directly in the interaction among family members. The antisocial behaviors then generalize from home to other settings, leading to social failures that in turn contribute to the long-term maintenance of the child in the antisocial process. (Patterson, Capaldi, & Bank, 1991, p. 139)

For anyone reading this who also happens to be a parent, this outcome might sting a little; at least, that was *my* first reaction. Initially, I interpreted Patterson as saying "Parents screw up their kids." Once the sting wore off, however, I actually came to love this statement. After reading Patterson's work, I totally understand and appreciate where he is coming from, even though it puts me as a parent directly in his crosshairs.

After spending a little time mulling over his studies, I've come to realize a few things about Patterson. When you read his work and the extent of his observations, he is not simply identifying a tragic comedy of errors leading to prison. However, I think his statement could use a bit of polish for everyday parents and practitioners. On that note, I'm going to reinterpret Patterson's statement based on my understanding of his research and his work:

> Parenting is hard. Sometimes as parents we make mistakes and accidentally reinforce (or build) negative behaviors in our kids. Most kids leave home to attend school, and the negative behavior learned at home goes to

school. Teaching is also hard. Sometimes as teachers we make mistakes and accidentally reinforce (or add on to) negative behaviors in our kids. These cascading effects interact with the child's individual temperament and personality. The series of interactions trigger a Frankenstein effect, creating a little monster. Little monsters don't make a lot of friends. Since friends and relationships help keep kids in check, a lack of those things can make kids get kinda weird. This weirdness often results in kids who start operating outside the norms and values of our environment. Once kids start operating outside of cultural and societal norms—they get busted. The problem with getting busted is that it does not help reform behavior. Getting busted only contributes to a seemingly nonstop cycle of pain and suffering.

There you have it. Yes, my version is a lot more verbose, but it's also less of an accusation, and I hope it helps clarify the profound observations made by Patterson without assigning any guilt to parents and teachers. To help his pupils and their sensitive egos along, Patterson eloquently described this entire process with a single word: *coercion*. You know my reference to the creation of little monsters? It's all coercion. In other words, when Luis slashed my face like a feral cat, Luis was being coercive.

COERCION IS A FOUR-LETTER WORD

Coercion is a gamble. Coercion is risky. Coercion is doing whatever it takes to improve your odds. Coercion is responding with the most shocking, crazy, scary behavior when you don't get your way. Coercion is an immediate explosion of rage and intimidation. Coercion is aggression with an agenda. Coercion is the reason kids act out.

Strangely enough, kids mostly stumble into coercion; they don't *mean* to become coercive. Sure, once they figure it out, they use it just like any other tool.

How could this be? you ask. *Why would caring adults allow their child to become a little monster?*

RANDOM REINFORCEMENT

After reviewing countless hours of coded parent–child behavioral interactions, Patterson confirmed that random reinforcement played a role in the development and maintenance of aggressive behavior in children. What is random reinforcement, then? The technical, jargon-rich explanation is something like "an intermittent conditioning schedule based on random or unpredictable reinforcement." This is such an important concept that I want to make sure we have the same understanding, particularly of the way Patterson has identified the role of random reinforcement. The most accessible analogy for random reinforcement is a slot machine. At first glance, the slot machine is a silly little box with windows and a lever. It doesn't look like any sort of teacher or trainer. Yet that little box is an excellent teacher and trainer. It can get adult men and women to enter a noisy (sometimes smelly) room, sit on an uncomfortable chair, pull a lever, and keep feeding it money. The slot machine actually teaches some complex patterns of behavior (e.g., entering a room, sitting down, inserting money in a designated sequence, pulling a lever, waiting, and repeating). How does a silly little box do so much teaching and training? It uses the jackpot (aka random reinforcement) response. It is almost paradoxical that the slot machine works *because* it is so consistently random. It teaches a complex sequence of behaviors because it is random. There is no consistent pattern to the slot machine's jackpot. In casinos, the jackpot is a bunch of money. It is no surprise that money is an extremely powerful reward for adults—particularly large sums of money all at once. Winning a jackpot or lottery or bet can be euphoric for people. The slot machine works only because the payoff is meaningful to adults. If the jackpot resulted in a box of oranges or a bag of socks, I don't think too many people would be drawn to slot machines. The payoff has to resonate and scratch an itch.

The behavioral mechanism behind the slot machine's jackpot is the same mechanism behind coercion. However, instead of slot machines, we are talking about parents and teachers. Instead of large sums of money, we're talking about jackpots for kids (e.g., getting out of work, getting what they want, staying home from school).

So are parents and teachers really just as consistently random as slot machines? According to Patterson, you bet. We may think that our lives are almost too routine and predictable, yet when we reflect on the nature of parenthood and teaching, there is nothing routine about it.

CONSISTENTLY INCONSISTENT

During a break at a parent training presentation, a mother of three shared with me her thoughts related to parenting. She felt that she had been a different parent to each of her three children. For instance, she said she'd had completely different outlooks on parenting and child-rearing for each child based on where she was in her life circumstances (e.g., newlywed, working mom, single mom). I was struck by this observation.

Clearly, this mother was the same person to all her children; however, based on her varied life stages plus the varied stages of parenthood, she took on different roles and perspectives as life and time trudged on. As a result, each of her children interacted with their mother in a variety of different ways and vice versa.

While this may sound like some sort of complex phenomenon, it is quite normal. The only thing we can expect in this life is unexpectedness. As such, while we may participate in daily routines, there is nothing routine about our lives. They are in constant flux, and most of us are making things up as we go along. Pretty random, right?

Due to this constant flux, we are not always prepared when a child decides to have a meltdown in the grocery store or at a family party. Our unpreparedness leads to inconsistent responses to our children's behaviors. These inconsistent responses are the basis of the random reinforcement Patterson identified in parent–child interactions. In other words, most of the time our parenting styles are random and inconsistent. Our inconsistent responses accidentally reward (or provide jackpots to) the child melting down at the grocery store.

This whole dynamic is not just reserved for parents. Teachers and educators can struggle with the exact same thing. Inconsistent responses from a teacher accidentally reward students melting down in the classroom, too.

THE COERCIVE CYCLE

With the understanding that each of us can fall into consistently inconsistent patterns of parenting and teaching, we are equipped to understand the driving force behind what Patterson has identified as the coercive cycle. Patterson's coercive cycle (see Figure 1) really is the answer to why aggression (a) develops so early in childhood, (b) becomes so problematic, and (c) persists into adulthood.

Figure 1 illustrates the complex interaction in a relatively simple manner. After the child explodes in a nuclear rage (Step 6), the parent and/or teacher may either give up (Step 7) or freak out (Step 8). Steps 7 and 8 are where the random reinforcement takes place. When the child explodes in Step 6, they are actually pulling the lever on the slot machine. The child is gambling that their parent or teacher will either give up or freak out. Additionally, just by exploding in a nuclear rage, the child avoids the initial request; so whether the parent or teacher gives up or freaks out, the odds are pretty high that the child will avoid the initial request. When the child becomes coercive, parents and teachers become more reluctant to make requests, and why wouldn't they? Their last request launched a nuclear warhead into the sporting goods section of Walmart! So inevitably, parents and teachers expose the child to fewer demands. In turn, the child has less and less practice responding appropriately to a request. We basically remove the child's ability to improve by limiting their opportunities to be successful. It's nothing short of madness! Yet it happens every day. How do we stop it

Figure 1 Patterson's Coercive Cycle

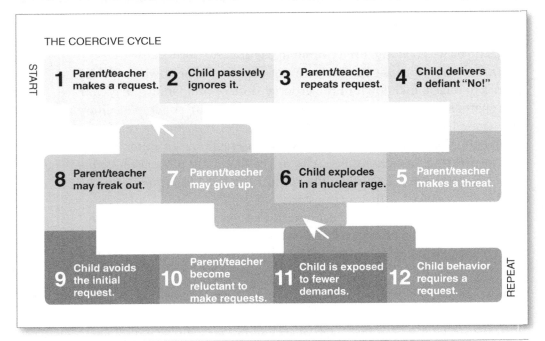

Created using the Venngage Infographic maker, https://venngage.com/

though? How do we actually create more opportunities for the child to respond to requests? How do we break the cycle?

BREAKING THE COERCIVE CYCLE

It has been my experience that the only way to break the coercive cycle is to (a) understand the behavior, (b) have a plan for that behavior, and (c) stick to that plan for the behavior. Hopefully, by surveying the roots of aggression and Patterson's work, we have accomplished the first step in understanding the behavior. What do we understand?

- Aggression exists because of our environments and our genetic predispositions.
- Chronic aggression is typically the result of coercion—a dynamic, cyclical process involving children, their parents, their teachers, and everybody else.
- The driving force behind this cycle is random reinforcement—or inconsistency.

In Chapter 7, we will cover in explicit detail how to create a plan addressing the aggressive behavior. The plan will include the tried-and-true principles of Applied Behavior Analysis, and data-based decision making and plan refinement. We will discuss the importance of sticking to a plan regardless of how silly it sounds. We will also discuss that any behavior plan worth implementing will need constant revision. In other words, successful behavior plans never look the same from start to finish. Behavior plans should be dynamic and fluid. However, this does not mean that we should stick to some exhausting dog-and-pony show of a behavior plan. I think it is an excellent practice to look at behavior plans the way Michelangelo looked at blocks of marble:

> *The true work of art is but a shadow of the divine perfection. I saw the angel in the marble and carved until I set him free. The greater danger for most of us lies not in setting our aim too high and falling short; but in setting our aim too low and achieving our mark.*

Our behavior intervention plans must be clear in our minds prior to drafting them. We must know exactly what behaviors we want to see at the end of the plan. We should not settle for the most immediate gain or removal of discomfort. While certainly there is room for those goals in our plans, they should go beyond the basics of on-task behavior, compliance, and work completion. Our plans should seek to set up the path to fulfillment and happiness as well. Also, just as Michelangelo never expected to complete a sculpture in 9 months, neither should you. Marble sculpting and meaningful behavior change take roughly the same amount of time (3 years). Set the stage with your school team by explaining that good plans require a marathon state of mind as opposed to a sprint state of mind. You may also work to put your school team at ease by acknowledging that behavior plans are refined and chipped away at in 2-week chunks. That's right. The *Happy Kids* approach recommends behavior plan monitoring every 2 weeks (10 school days)! This allows for plenty of collaboration and communication regarding the success of the approach. It also gives us time to actually stick to something. It has been my experience that sticking to a lackluster plan consistently is always better than implementing a stellar plan inconsistently. Consistency is the Kryptonite to randomness. Randomness and inconsistency are the driving forces of coercion. Coercion is at the root of aggression in our youth. Our kids deserve some consistency, and so do you.

As stated earlier, we will cover how to draft an excellent behavior intervention plan in Chapter 7. Prior to that step, however, we need to make sure that we have gotten rid of any bad tools in our behavioral toolbox.

We have to jettison the approaches that simply do not work. We cannot move forward with a solid, positive, and effective behavior plan if we include stuff that doesn't work. The next chapter will briefly review what does not work in reducing aggression. Therefore, you will have been warned. If you attempt any of these strategies flagged as ineffective (and in some cases harmful), you will be ineffective and you may cause harm. Inefficacy and harm are not consistent with the *Happy Kids* approach. So the next chapter will identify these archaic practices and interpretations and then throw them in the trash once and for all.

READY-TO-USE TOOLS (CHAPTER 1)

I. **The Coercive Cycle and How to Break It! (Appendix A)**

    <u>What:</u> An infographic central to the concepts covered in Chapter 1 (as well as specific steps for how to break the coercive cycle).

    <u>Why:</u> The more people with whom you work who understand this cycle, the better. It is crucial to understand this process prior to attempting to break the cycle.

    <u>How to use it right now:</u> Use this graphic as both a prophetic warning for parents and teachers and as an explanation for why a target student engages in nuclear-rage tantrums. This concept is central to understanding, preventing, and responding to dangerous and/or aggressive behavior. The more comfortable you are explaining the coercive cycle and the more people you can help understand it and how to break it, the better.

What Does Not Work

2

Man must evolve a method which rejects revenge, aggression, and retaliation. The foundation of such a method is love.

—Martin Luther King Jr. (1967)

I was desperate. It had been a rough couple of weeks working with Annie, a 9-year-old girl who could explode at the drop of a hat. Her most recent tantrum had resulted in the destruction of every last one of Mrs. Slater's antique tape recorders. Mrs. Slater had been using the recorders religiously for student read-alongs for the previous 20 years. Needless to say, Mrs. Slater had had it with Annie. (If I was being honest, I had had it, too.) Annie knew better, but she was deeply entrenched in a coercive cycle. Looking back at that time period with Annie, I'm positive she was constantly upping her ante in the coercion gamble. It was as if she were shopping for what would break us, constantly on the lookout. Annie's visits to the office of Mr. Rodriguez, the school principal, were becoming increasingly regular, even daily events. Mr. Rodriguez was also losing his patience and began mulling over the idea of long-term suspension. When Annie got wind of Mr. Rodriguez's threats of suspension, she took it personally. She would get upset at the very mention of his name.

As I sat in my office, my e-mail chimed an alert. It was Annie's private therapist, a licensed psychologist. In the subject line of her e-mail, she wrote: *I've got it!*

Finally, after weeks of collaborating with all of Annie's stakeholders, this could be the payoff! I anxiously scrolled through the e-mail, skimming the contents. Then I paused and reread it more deliberately. Could this be for real? Below is an exact copy of the e-mail:

To: Ben Springer
cc: [Annie's Mom]
Subject: I've got it!

Hey Ben,

I think we had a breakthrough today in therapy that I'm excited to share with you. After visiting with Annie for the past few weeks, she seemed to be fixated on Mr. Rodriguez, her principal. She was so angry every time his name was mentioned. Apparently Mr. Rodriguez called home last week and Annie did not like getting in trouble like that. So, we printed out a picture of Mr. Rodriguez and I gathered up five tennis balls. We taped up the picture and I had Annie throw the tennis balls at the picture. At first, she was kinda shy about it, but then she got really into it. And get this—after we were done (about 15 minutes or so), she said, "I feel so much better! Can we do this again?" Can you believe it? It was so cathartic for her!

I think you could do the same exercise in your office. We could track her aggression at school before and after the "tennis ball intervention." Let me know.

[Name Omitted]
—Licensed Psychologist

There is a wonderful White Stripes song called "I'm Lonely (but I Ain't That Lonely Yet)." The song jumped into my head as soon as I read this e-mail. I was desperate for some ideas to help Annie, but I wasn't that desperate yet. Honestly, I was shocked. I had nothing but respect for this therapist and knew she was just trying to help, but this was off the mark of what we knew about Annie—and way off the mark of what we know about human behavior. Annie's psychologist was recommending a treatment based in catharsis theory. This theory posits that venting anger will produce a positive improvement in an individual's psychological state, thereby reducing levels of aggression. According to this view, anger and aggression live inside us, like an energy. If the energy is not released, it builds and builds until it explodes, resulting in aggression. Sounds logical, right? Well, as it turns out, this theory has been debunked quite extensively since Sigmund Freud created it. In 1977, researchers Geen and Quanty actually found the opposite to be true. Their participants became *more* aggressive when allowed to act out aggressively. Their study's findings have been replicated over and over again. In one clever study, Bushman, Baumeister, and Phillips (2001) found that while aggressing does not reduce subsequent aggression, people may nonetheless believe that venting and aggressing will make them feel better. In other words, catharsis doesn't reduce aggression, but because we think it does, we keep doing it.

I could conduct my own research on catharsis theory every Sunday in the fall when I watch the NFL. If catharsis worked on aggression, I could expect some significant behavior changes as the season progresses. Imagine week four in the NFL season if catharsis worked. The players might be scrapbooking instead of charging after their opponents, inflicting crushing blows. Yet we know that week four NFL football games have zero scrapbooking and plenty of high-speed, jarringly violent aggression. In fact, the intensity of the games seems to increase as the season progresses.

I did not print a picture of Mr. Rodriguez, nor did I instruct Annie to "get her aggression out" by throwing balls at the principal's face. I was still pretty stunned by the therapist's recommendation. I began to grapple with the notion of how someone with a level of training similar to my own could possibly recommend a treatment that does not work. Unfortunately, a bunch of other professionals probably would, too. So I made an effort to track down the practices parents and schools use that simply do not work. This chapter comprises a complete review of the practices I have discovered. I will do my best to bury these practices forever under mounds of research and common sense. May they rest in peace.

RIP CORPORAL PUNISHMENT

While corporal punishment might appear to be a thing of the past, the idea of using corporal punishment to thwart difficult student behavior is still floating around. I kid you not, every year, at least once a year, I hear a colleague provide the following proposition: "You know what that kid really needs, dontcha? A swift kick in the ass!" Seriously. The idea of hitting kids to "set them straight" still gets passed around.

But corporal punishment does not work in reducing aggression. Smacking a kid after they smack you doesn't work. Spanking a child on the bottom does not work. I'd like this message to reach the 50% of parents with toddlers and 68% of parents with preschoolers in the United States who still use corporal punishment as a regular method of discipline (Regalado, Sareen, Inkelas, Wissow, & Halfon, 2004; Socolar, Savage, & Evans, 2007).

Did you know that by the time children in the United States reach middle and high school, 85% have been physically punished by their parents (Bender et al., 2007)? That is a lot of spanking (or worse) for nothing. Not only does corporal punishment not work, but it can actually contribute to more aggression in children (Gershoff, 2002). It is harmful and models aggressive acts for children. There is no reason corporal punishment should exist anywhere. Working with children struggling with aggression is difficult enough without anyone contributing to the problem.

Finally, I hope my conclusion is glaringly obvious: If corporal punishment doesn't work at home, it certainly doesn't work at school. In 1987, a formal organization called the National Coalition to Abolish Corporal Punishment in Schools was developed. The coalition included the National Center on Child Abuse Prevention, the American Academy of Pediatrics, the American Bar Association, the American Medical Association, the Parent-Teacher Association, the National Education Association, the Society for Adolescent Medicine, and over 20 other groups that were united in their efforts to ban the practice of hurting children physically as a form of punishment. In a pitch-perfect position paper in the *Journal of Adolescent Health*, the Society for Adolescent Medicine made the following statement:

> *Physically punishing children has never been shown to enhance moral character development, increase the students' respect for teachers or other authority figures in general, intensify the teacher's control in class, or even protect the teacher. Such children, in our view, are being physically and mentally abused and no data exist demonstrating that such victims develop enhanced social skills or self-control skills.* (Greydanus et al., 2003, p. 388)

This sort of statement is not forceful, revolutionary, or bold; it is common sense. And I applaud the positions outlined in this paper. It is incredible that our laws prevent adults from physically hurting other adults but not from physically hurting children as punishment. This goes beyond some archaic practice that is not effective. This is about how we should treat our children and each other. Absolutely nothing good has come from this type of punishment. We need to evolve and take children's needs more seriously. Share this passage with every educator with whom you come in contact. RIP corporal punishment. Ashes to ashes and dust to dust.

RIP REPRIMANDS

Telling a child to stop hitting does not stop them from hitting. Scolding a child for hitting does not prevent hitting. Nagging at children to stop hitting does not work, either. Calling a child out in front of their peers does not work. For whatever reason, some parents and a lot of teachers do not make use of positive strategies such as ongoing praise for positive behavior. Instead, they actually use coercion to deal with aggressive student behavior! Can you believe it? Parents and teachers will use threats, nags, and/or reprimands (Shores, Gunter, & Jack, 1993; Van Acker, 2007) despite how ineffective they are. In fact, by choosing to be coercive, these parents and teachers actually worsen the behaviors they are trying to stop.

There are so many options to help prevent and alter negative behavior. None involve the use of reprimands. I know that every once in a while you may need to give a reprimand, and reprimands certainly can roll off the tongue. If you have to use a reprimand, O'Leary, Kaufman, Kass, and Drabman (1970) have provided some direction: Keep it quiet, private, and brief. If you really want to add a little sugar to your spice, include a reminder regarding the expected behavior. A reprimand should never be simply a reprimand; it should be a teaching moment. (Appendix D provides you with "The Better Reprimand," a method to deliver reprimands to students that avoids harm and makes space for a teaching moment.)

RIP SUSPENSION/EXPULSION

What's that? you say. Public schools' de facto use of discipline doesn't work to reduce aggression? In fact, suspension doesn't work at all? It's true. Nor do zero-tolerance policies. That's right, the bread and butter of school-based discipline does nothing at all to reduce aggression. While a lot of school boards continue to believe their zero-tolerance policies are tough and they purposefully increase the intensity of consequences for all offenders, they really just end up being heavy-handed. This imbalance of discipline has led to indiscriminate use of school district resources. Consider the implications associated with expulsions: Students may get expelled for anything, from the misuse of paper clips to minor fighting, or even the possession of organic cough drops (Skiba, 1999). In my role as an administrator, I've been on the phone trying to explain some of these scenarios. Kids do weird stuff—don't get me wrong—but there are lots of better ways to help correct their behavior than kicking them out of school. (Spoiler alert: There are tons of successful methods, and most of them are in this book.)

I remember being called to the office of a somber principal to discuss the discipline of a third grader. When I arrived, the principal and her cabinet of teachers and secretary sat solemnly around the table. I was told a 9-year-old had brought a knife wrapped in a hand towel to school. The principal ceremoniously unwrapped the towel revealing a butter knife.

My first reaction was to laugh, but of course I didn't, because I understand that bringing a knife to school is serious business. However, my problem was that there were a lot of people in the principal's office staring blankly at a butter knife that day, none of whom had any real idea what to do beyond some sort of disciplinary protocol. When asked my opinion, my concerns had absolutely nothing to do with a knife on campus but with *why* this little 9-year-old boy had brought it. I did not want to discipline the child; I didn't even know the child, but I wanted to help him. I wanted to find out what he was trying to communicate to his peers and those of us standing in the room. I could not see any good in suspending the student when (as far as I could tell) he was less dangerous than he was in need of our attention and compassion. What would we be demonstrating to this 9-year-old and his family if we suspended him? You don't fit in here? Go back home and think about what you did? C'mon, this is the 21st century! We know so much about kids and why they do the things they do. Archaic practices like suspensions, expulsions, and zero-tolerance policies should be left behind. That chapter of goofy discipline should be closed for good.

As it turned out, the child was in desperate need of attention and was experiencing significant stress and anxiety not only at school but at home as well. In his efforts to cope with the stress and anxiety of his life, he had very few models of appropriate coping mechanisms. It was reasonable to conclude that bringing the butter knife to school helped him feel in control of something. After interviewing him, I learned he had no intention of ever using the knife; he said it made him feel safe, that's all.

School disciplinary data at both the district (Skiba, Peterson, & Williams, 1997) and national (Heaviside, Rowland, Williams, & Farris, 1998) levels have shown that the serious infractions that are the primary targets of zero tolerance (e.g., drugs, weapons, gangs) occur relatively infrequently. The most frequent disciplinary events with which schools wrestle are minor disruptive behaviors such as tardiness, class absence, disrespect, and noncompliance.

I am not saying that the solutions are simple; I am just saying that zero tolerance and the de facto suspension/expulsion game don't work (Bain & Macpherson, 1990; Cooley, 1995; Skiba et al., 1997). To date, there is no evidence that zero-tolerance policies make a difference; so regardless of the message they send, zero-tolerance policies are ineffective (Borgwald & Theixos, 2013).

The most effective alternatives to suspension include the following two approaches: (1) good old-fashioned instruction and (2) awareness of the core beliefs of stakeholders and the child. These alternatives are not sexy, but they are why schools are so well equipped to manage difficult behavior.

Within each of our school buildings are a bunch of teachers—teachers who know how to teach. With just a little bit of guidance, teachers can teach positive student behavior. I know they can, because I have always considered teaching reading and math much more complicated than teaching positive behavior. If teachers can do that stuff, they can teach positive behavior. As such, it is important to work with our teacher teams and administrators to liken behavioral instruction to academic instruction. Can you imagine kicking a student out of school because they struggle reading? (I can't, either.) It is difficult to imagine, because the core belief of most educators is that children can learn and grow.

Now, identifying core beliefs is not just something you jump into. It takes some "warming up," and, well, you may not have a lot of extra time, so Appendix F provides a graphic illustrating how to understand "core beliefs" of kids (or of anyone, really). Essentially, when faced with some sort of necessary response or discipline, consider how the response will affect the student's (and the team's) self-esteem, self-efficacy, and self-worth. If we seek to provide a response that improves the self-esteem, self-efficacy, and self-worth of a student, alternatives to suspension will manifest themselves.

All that being said, when applied judiciously, suspensions may play a role in helping students. The primary role suspension can play is to allow a sort of gathering of wits or gathering of ducks to be put in a row. What I mean is that administrators and school teams faced with dangerous behavior don't get a lot of notice or time prior to a behavioral crisis. As such, having a brief time period to get organized and allocate resources can come in handy. There have been times when a basic day (or two) helped the team and me by giving us some breathing room to draft more appropriate supports for the student. It is my opinion that any/all suspensions should coincide with a refined behavior plan with explicit details for the team to prevent and respond to misbehavior.

MOVING FORWARD

As we shed crocodile tears for the passing of ineffective (and potentially harmful) practices, let's look forward to greener pastures. I'd feel silly rejecting a series of practices without offering solutions. The remainder of this book is dedicated to sharing solutions that not only work but actually contribute to helping children (and the adults with whom they work) find happiness. We will attempt to follow Martin Luther King Jr.'s admonition, "Man must evolve a method which rejects revenge, aggression, and retaliation. The foundation of such a method is love." If you feel the slightest discomfort using the word *love* in connection with discipline, school, and student safety, just use the word *compassion*. The foundation of the best approaches for students is compassion.

READY-TO-USE TOOLS (CHAPTER 2)

I. **RIP Catharsis (Appendix B)**

<u>What:</u> A graphic explaining catharsis and why it is not an effective treatment for aggression.

<u>Why:</u> You simply never know when you will have to share evidence with stakeholders. It is nice to have something that is visual, simple, and detailed on hand to explain why you have ruled out an approach.

<u>How to use it right now:</u> Share the graphic with stakeholders in a respectful manner. Explain that it came with a book describing best practices in the treatment of aggression.

II. **RIP Corporal Punishment (Appendix C)**

<u>What:</u> A resource designed to be shared with parents, teachers, and administrators, complete with alternative approaches with better outcomes for students.

<u>Why:</u> We are all so busy, quick reference guides with authentic research can be helpful tools. In fact, the cuter, more colorful, and shinier the better. People see so much black-and-white text all day, it is amazing what a little color can bring to a communication.

<u>How to use it right now:</u> Share the resource with stakeholders in a respectful manner. Explain that modern-day school systems reject corporal punishment—and for good reason. Explain that in rejecting corporal punishment, the stage is set for more respectful communication and meaningful relationships with children.

III. **The Better Reprimand (Appendix D)**

<u>What:</u> Steps to complete a flawless reprimand.

<u>Why:</u> You will undoubtedly need to correct a student's behavior. You may be tempted to use a reprimand instead of something like differential reinforcement (see Appendix E). When you do, make it private, quiet, and brief. Sprinkle in some reminders of behavior expectations and you'll be on your way to better reprimands!

How to use it right now: Study the steps diligently, and then give it a whirl! Take inventory on how it went and what you could do to improve and refine your delivery.

IV. **Differential Reinforcement of Incompatible Behavior (DRI) (Appendix E)**

What: This is a reference tool with steps to complete DRI in your classroom, on the bus, and beyond.

Why: "The Better Reprimand" is good but may not even be necessary if you are actively enlisting DRI. DRI keeps the focus on behaviors you want to see students exhibit.

How to use it right now: Review the steps of DRI and practice them when you are tempted to use a reprimand. When a student is misbehaving and your redirection isn't working, praise the behavior you want to see in other children nearby.

V. **Identifying Core Beliefs When Considering Discipline (Appendix F)**

What: An illustration to help administrators, teachers, and parents remember what the big picture is when disciplining a student.

Why: When faced with disciplinary decisions, reminding ourselves of the stakeholders and the child of their core beliefs will help guide our decision making.

How to use it right now: In an effort to "warm up" the discussion for you and stakeholders surrounding core beliefs and how to liken behavior management to academic instruction, share the illustration and help the team identify what is at the center of the next steps in discipline for the student.

The Triangle
of Power
Systems of
Prevention and You

An ounce of prevention is worth a pound of cure.

—Benjamin Franklin (1706–1790)

I have heard hospital employees joke about the connection between a full moon and an increase in bizarre patient dilemmas. (There has been no proof of a causal connection, as investigated by the *Annals of Emergency Medicine* [Coates, Dietrich, & Cottington, 1989] and the *Indian Journal of Medical Sciences* [Zargar et al., 2004]; I just think it's funny.)

Educators have a similar joke about the effects of Halloween. It is widely said that students become "possessed" around October 31. (Add a full moon and look out!) I have not seen any research in this area, but I had one week leading up to Halloween that made me wonder.

In any given school year, I may be the point person for 15 or so students struggling with behavioral and emotional problems. Inevitably, I prioritize these students on a scale of intensity. This scale usually leaves me with five (or so) students struggling with some really difficult behavior problems. However, in my efforts to closely monitor my "top five," my ability to monitor the other students gradually wanes as I go down the line. Needless to say, this is always a balancing act. Well, this tiny house of cards was destroyed on Friday, October 30, the day before Halloween. I am willing to relive this trauma only to help illustrate the importance—the necessity—of prevention when it comes to managing aggressive student behavior. It is astounding what can go wrong when there is not a universal method of prevention. Exhibit A: Friday, October 30.

FRIDAY, OCTOBER 30

I was on a routine follow-up in Mrs. Livingston's classroom. I wanted to check in with a 13-year-old female named Chrissie. Chrissie had been diagnosed in early childhood with an autism spectrum disorder. She had a lovely singing voice but could explode into nuclear rages if the lunch menu changed. Chrissie was taller and heavier than her peers, so when she acted out aggressively, it was dangerous and unsettling to witness. We had worked as a team to build "Chrissie blueprints" complete with "uh-oh plans" to help her prepare and cope with the stress of unexpected menu changes. Things were going well for a week or so, until that day, unexpectedly, the cafeteria ran out of green slushy drinks and began serving red slushy drinks. When Chrissie saw a student pass her classroom with a red slushy, she began pacing anxiously and said something like, "Uh-oh plans are stupid! Uh-oh plans do *not* work!" With one look, Mrs. Livingston communicated with me telepathically, *Close that door!* So I gently closed the door. Chrissie was only slightly less stressed when she noticed the door was closed, blocking her view of red-slushy-carrying passersby.

At that very moment, my cell phone buzzed. It was a frantic text explaining that Gentry, a kindergartner in my "top five" had locked himself in the faculty restroom. The principal could not locate the keys to the restroom and was growing concerned, not knowing if they should wait it out or call the custodian, or even call the police. I texted back (with one eye on Chrissie) that they should contact the police if the custodian did not arrive immediately.

Gentry was not your average kindergartner. He was a cute little kid, but he didn't sleep very well and didn't eat very well. His parents had been trying for years to understand why, but he just had difficulty sleeping and apparently ate only cheese quesadillas. Due to this lack of sleep and tummy trouble, Gentry's aggressive outbursts were incredibly intense. When he got angry, the look in his eyes was almost feral. The fact that he was in a bathroom unsupervised was alarming to me.

I communicated telepathically to Mrs. Livingston, *Hey, do you think Chrissie is okay? I gotta leave and check on another student.* To which Mrs. Livingston responded, *Don't you dare leave me here with Chrissie and these godforsaken red slushies.* (Telepathy is all in the eyes.)

As I stood in the classroom pondering my next steps, I thumbed through the e-mails on my phone. Mrs. Claven had marked an e-mail with a red exclamation point and given it the subject line: *Beep Tape is Not Working!* I had introduced a beep tape into Mrs. Claven's classroom the previous week to help her manage Tyrone. Tyrone was a fifth grader who would do just about anything for attention from adults and peers. A beep tape is a strategy that enlists an interval (fixed or intermittent) schedule to remind the adults in the room to catch target students engaging in positive behavior at a higher rate than negative behavior. I had shared the beep tape concept with Mrs. Claven to help her give Tyrone the attention he wanted, but on her terms.

I don't know if it was the tension or stress I was feeling, but against my better judgement, I opened Mrs. Claven's e-mail. Mrs. Claven had composed what appeared to be a novel about the 101 reasons she needed more support for Tyrone in her classroom. She blasted the use of the beep tape by saying that she was "not Pavlov's dog" and that Tyrone actually needed one-on-one support or he simply "would wither on the vine and perish."

Clearly, I was distracted by the e-mail, because I lost sight of Chrissie. When I looked up from my phone, she was glaring out the window in the door with tears welling up in her eyes. These were not tears of sadness; they were tears of rage and pre-emotional combustion. My phone vibrated. Gentry had kicked the door open, injuring the custodian. My phone vibrated again. Tyrone had pulled his pants down and mooned a group of girls at recess. Chrissie pounded her fist on the door. My phone vibrated again and again and again! The e-mails and texts I was receiving were for all 15 students in my caseload. Halloween had come a day early and I simply could not respond to all the tricks and treats the students were presenting.

The onslaught of phone calls, texts, and e-mails and the demands of my current situation became too much for me. I am pretty sure this experience is common with other professionals in similar roles. A caseload of students struggling with emotional and behavioral problems is never a breeze to manage, and every once in a while, the caseload can become *too* tricky.

My insides wouldn't stop churning that Friday. I never even left Mrs. Livingston's classroom. Chrissie had a pretty serious meltdown, scattering classroom supplies and tipping over desks. The texts and e-mails just piled up, not to mention the fallout of parent voicemails about Gentry and Tyrone. When I finally left Mrs. Livingston and Chrissie's school, the sun was setting and revealed a massive yellow moon. If I were a superstitious person, I would have chalked that day up to Halloween and the full moon. It was too strange, too crazy, and too scary to be anything else, right?

Well, I am *not* a superstitious person. I knew what the problem was: I was putting out fires instead of preventing them. I had gotten stuck in a reactionary cycle. Teachers and parents were getting too dependent on responsive services—and could I blame them? I was not contributing to a feedback loop in my district. I was in the trenches, on the front lines, and I was not relaying the status back to headquarters! I was stuck in my own little crisis–response–crisis–response cycle, and nothing was getting better. As silly as it may seem, I finally realized I could not be everywhere at once. There had to be a better way.

ENTER THE TRIANGLE OF POWER

The better way for each of us has come in the shape of a triangle. I was so busy that I had forgotten about the triangle. My student caseload was keeping me so preoccupied that I had lost sight of the big picture—the big triangle. What is this big triangle? The triangle is the symbol of prevention in schools. For the past 15 years, the triangle has been at the heart of every training program involving behavioral intervention and academic instruction in modern-day school systems. Without fail, every single one of those training sessions has included a graphic of a green-yellow-and-red triangle. If you were an alien from outer space visiting educational trainings, I am pretty sure you would return to your home planet reporting that educators on the planet Earth consider the triangle to be some sort of educational deity. This is not good or bad; it's just the way it is. The triangle has dominated educational reform and philosophy for many years. For that reason, I refer to it as the Triangle of Power. This triangle comes in an insane number of variations, but they all look something like Figure 2.

THE HISTORY OF THE TRIANGLE OF POWER

We can trace the origins of the Triangle of Power back to the 1980s, when research institutions experienced a reinvigorated interest in determining the effectiveness of behavioral strategies in the school setting (Baer, 1985; Cullinan, Epstein, & McLinden, 1986; Gresham, 1991; Hersh & Walker, 1983). Results of these investigations recommended a stronger commitment from school psychologists to identify evidence-based practices, conduct functional assessments on problem behavior, and avoid the trappings of purely "diagnostic" classification systems.

Based on these results, Gresham (1991) called for a reconceptualization of "behavior disorders" to move beyond a basic "disturbed/not disturbed" framework and include a "resistance to intervention" framework. In other words, instead of simply identifying and labeling students when

Figure 2   The Triangle of Power

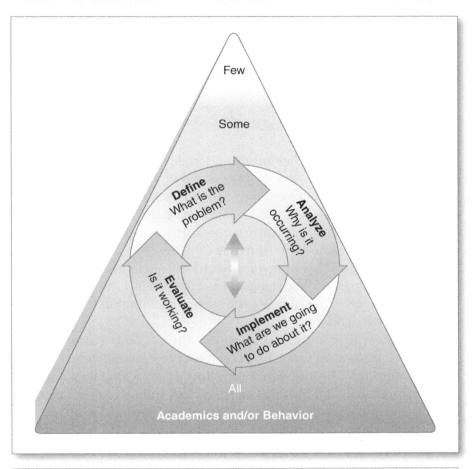

Created using the Venngage Infographic maker, https://venngage.com/

they acted out, why not attempt a series of effective interventions and monitor a child's individual response to said intervention? This framework placed the onus on the skills and training of the practitioner over the individual characteristics of the student.

After the reinvigorated interest in student response (or resistance) to behavioral intervention of the 1980s, the 1990s heralded the reauthorization of the Individuals with Disabilities Education Act (IDEA) of 1997. This act legislated the dissemination and provision of technical assistance on evidence-based practices in schools, for improving behavioral disorders among students, and led to a unique collaboration of researchers and implementers from the Universities of Oregon, Kansas, Kentucky, Missouri, and South Florida. These researchers established the modern-day basis for Multi-Tiered Systems of Support (MTSS) in the form of the Positive Behavioral Interventions and Supports (PBIS) Center. MTSS is defined as a framework for enhancing the adoption and implementation of a continuum of evidence-based interventions to achieve academically and behaviorally important outcomes for all students (Sugai et al., 2000).

THE TRIANGLE OF POWER IN ACTION

The theory and practice behind the Triangle of Power (aka PBIS, aka MTSS) involve four components: (1) systematic use of assessment data, (2) efficient allocation of resources, (3) enhanced learning, and (4) applicability for all children. The whole idea behind the Triangle of Power is that educators will enlist proactive strategies to help children rather than waiting for problems to arise (Burns & Gibbons, 2008; Sugai & Horner, 1999; Tilly, 2003). These four components are organized into three tiers (which the Triangle of Power illustrates quite well). Table 1 shows how these tiers are applied. (They are the same tiers found in every triangle graphic known to man.)

For a closer look at these tiers, we must turn to the dynamic duo of school-wide positive behavior supports: George Sugai and Robert Horner (2015). Sugai and Horner have been at this gig for a long time and have made exceptional strides with a broad reach of influence over individual schools and districts across the United States and beyond.

Table 1 The Three Tiers

Tier	Percentage of Student Population	Description	Frequency of Assessment
1	All students	Universal: Adherence to a research-based core curriculum in general education	Benchmark assessment at least three times/year
2	About 15% of all students	Targeted: Small-group (three to five students) interventions delivered as part of general education	At least monthly progress monitoring
3	About 5% of all students	Intensive: Individualized interventions based on problem-solving models; could include special education services	At least weekly progress monitoring and frequent informal classroom-based assessments

Sugai and Horner Talk Tier 1

Sugai and Horner describe Tier 1 as "primary prevention." They suggest that this tier must be understood as proactive and designed to be administered prior to the occurrence of any aggressive behavior. Because all students receive Tier 1 supports, the practices must be highly efficient and logically integrated with all other elements of the environment.

Sugai and Horner Talk Tier 2

Sugai and Horner describe Tier 2 as "secondary prevention." This second tier must moderately increase the intensity of student supports to address the most common needs of students with ongoing aggression. They suggest that the elevated level of risk experienced by these students should be matched not only by elevated support but also by an increase in the frequency and specificity of progress-monitoring data.

Sugai and Horner Talk Tier 3

Sugai and Horner describe Tier 3 as "tertiary prevention." This third tier is characterized by individualized assessment and the management of support by a team uniquely organized to see the preferences and needs of the individual student. While these types of supports have been found for many years in special education, the value of Tier 3 supports extends beyond special education to all students requiring higher-intensity supports.

Thanks, Sugai and Horner! But what, exactly, does any of this triangle business have to do with my nightmare scenario on that fateful day before Halloween? What the heck does the Triangle of Power have to do with Chrissie's response to red slushies, Gentry's kicking a bathroom door, or Tyrone's pulling his pants down and mooning a group of girls? Everything.

PREVENTION IS THE BEST MEDICINE

My Halloween nightmare was not that different from the experiences of many other modern-day school practitioners. Modern-day educators are expected to do it all. They are asked to teach an increasingly diverse and heterogeneous student population (Lane, Wehby, & Robertson, 2008), maintain the rigor of high academic standards, and accommodate students of all abilities in inclusive settings (MacMillan, Gresham, & Forness, 1996).

The Halloween experience forced me to take inventory of the students with whom I was working and really evaluate who needed the most intensive services. In terms of the Triangle of Power, I needed to evaluate what I was doing at the tip of the triangle (you know, in the red area). As I broke down my caseload, it became increasingly clear that many of the students I was monitoring didn't necessarily require the intensive supports I offered. In fact, I was able to create a basic metric for the intensity and time spent with students. Based on this metric, there were kids who didn't require a ton of intensity or a ton of time. Sure, they required some sensitivities and behavior management, but for the most part, I think the students' teacher teams could have been effective in managing their behaviors.

Certainly, the Chrissies and the Gentrys require special, Tier 3 attention, but the Tyrones? I imagine that Tyrone's level of misbehavior could have been addressed with a Tier 2 or even Tier 1 behavior management strategy. That Halloween, I was forced to recognize how meaningless my efforts were without a system.

So when the Triangle of Power touts the benefits of MTSS, it is really touting three phases of prevention. Tier 1 may be considered universal prevention, or "prevention for all." Universal prevention is designed to prevent problems from occurring. Examples of universal prevention can be readily observed in every school in the United States. Prior to enrollment, schools require immunization records. This is a universal practice to help reduce the likelihood that children will contract harmful diseases like hepatitis, the flu, or whooping cough. In the academic arena, many schools provide universal reading screenings. These screenings act like universal blood tests. They're not diagnostic—they can't tell you what the problem is—but they can tell you if there *is* a problem with oral reading fluency and perhaps comprehension. Wouldn't it be great if there were such screening systems for behavioral, social, and emotional problems? (Spoiler alert: There *are* such screening systems.)

BEFORE SCREENING, FIND MEANING

When we have an understanding of MTSS and the associated process for addressing behavior problems, the next logical step is to consider universal screening for behavioral and emotional concerns. Prior to that step, it is really important to take an inventory of our individual school and/or district. Just because books like mine and research like this (Goodman, 1997; Gresham, MacMillan, Beebe-Frankenberger, & Bocain, 2000; Lane, Kalberg, Parks, & Carter, 2008; Lanyon, 2006; Walker & Severson, 1992) tout the importance and significance of screening doesn't mean it is simple.

The honest truth is that if systematic screening of behavioral and emotional concerns were simple, we'd all be doing it. In fact, the whole

MTSS process of implementation is pretty complex. There are a number of steps required to successfully implement MTSS (Fixsen, Blase, Naoom, & Duda, 2015). Seriously, there is this network called the National Implementation Research Network (NIRN), and according to NIRN, there are exactly 56 steps across three separate drivers—competency drivers, organization drivers, and leadership drivers—required to implement MTSS authentically.

I'm sure the folks at NIRN have it all figured out and their resources are very helpful. What I'm trying to communicate here is what I try to communicate to myself when I am dieting: We must be honest about our weaknesses. When I attempt a diet, I have to accept the fact that glazed apple fritters are my weakness. Apple fritters will always win against a healthier choice. So if I attempt to diet, I must avoid bakeries at all costs. If I don't take my weakness for apple fritters seriously, I set myself up to fail. The folks at NIRN include steps to this process (not for my addiction to apple fritters but for MTSS implementation) in their Hexagon Tool, which helps schools and districts avoid the bad setup. It is essentially a to-do list that keeps school districts on track by reminding them that MTSS must fit with current initiatives, organizational structure, and community values.

Likewise, if we don't accept our individual school/district's weaknesses prior to tackling a universal screening system, we will be setting up our school/district to fail. The idea, then, is to take it slow. There should be enough data within these pages to convince any school board or principal of the benefits of a universal screening system for behavioral and emotional problems. The next realistic and practical step is to meet your school district where it is when it comes to universal screening.

Prior to moving head-on into this world, evaluate the following practices and procedures:

- Does the school or district apply any other universal screening practices (e.g., immunizations, reading)?
- If so, how frequently does the school or district review the results of the screening practices?
- Universal screening procedures typically involve some sort of feedback loop. Can you or a school/district representative describe what this feedback loop looks like? For instance, what does the school/district look at and evaluate?
- Does the district have any resources to allocate to a continuum of services for behavioral and emotional problems? For instance, what will the school/district do when it successfully identifies students who would benefit from a small group of behavioral and/or

emotional skill instruction? What about students who may require one-on-one instruction?
* Does the school/district provide universal screening practices that are inclusive for all students with diverse languages and backgrounds?

If your school/district is firing on all cylinders with these bullet points, flip to Appendix G for a listing of all the evidence-based universal screening tools available for schools and districts. Pick any one of them and immediately infuse it directly into the other universal practices your school/district is implementing. High-functioning MTSS schools and districts possess the infrastructure to support all three tiers of support (i.e., all students, some students, few students) for academics and lend themselves nicely to integrating behavioral MTSS.

If your school/district is flirting with the idea of behavioral MTSS, flip to Appendix H for steps to implement a pilot study in your school or district. Pilot studies are excellent ways to try out an approach or new idea in a school system. The stakes are purposefully lower in this type of implementation; it is meant to provide practical experience for stakeholders interested in pursuing behavioral MTSS. Remember, MTSS is a complicated process of (1) systematic use of assessment data, (2) efficient allocation of resources, (3) enhanced learning, and (4) applicability for all children.

If your school/district has no clue what the heck MTSS is and just needs to start from scratch, increase attention and funding to professional development that includes school board members, district leadership, building leadership, faculty, and staff. Essentially, you will have to organize a big "Triangle of Power" party (feel free to use this book as your guide) to help explain why systems of prevention are necessary and really the most sustainable system to address behavioral and emotional problems in youths.

BEN FRANKLIN WAS RIGHT

When I came back to work after the Halloween weekend, on Monday, November 2, I had a new purpose, and it involved Ben Franklin's iconic admonition (with a few slight alterations): "An ounce of (MTSS) is worth a pound of (behavior plan)." Systems of prevention are a big deal, and if you don't have a principal (or district leadership) who (a) understands MTSS or (b) is willing to implement MTSS, you are all alone on an island. You will be stuck (as was I) in a constant crisis–response–crisis–response cycle. You will burn out, and there will be no improvement in student behavior.

Appendix I has some tips and tricks to engender administrator and team buy-in to the whole prevention/screening business. Remember, MTSS and the Triangle of Power don't have any conceptual problems; the theory and model behind MTSS and prevention are very solid. There are even steps to take that will help you and your school implement MTSS. The problem comes either when district and school leadership don't understand the complexity of MTSS in action or when it is simply not a priority for them. So take a quick inventory of your district's or school's interest in MTSS.

READY-TO-USE TOOLS (CHAPTER 3)

I. **List of Evidence-Based Screening Tools (Appendix G)**

<u>What:</u> A list of evidence-based screening tools to help schools and districts identify student emotional and behavioral needs *before* they become a problem.

<u>Why:</u> If you are working in a high-functioning MTSS school or district, there should be a pretty strong infrastructure to facilitate social/emotional/behavioral screening that leads to Tier 1 refinement, Tier 2 resources, and Tier 3 interventions/supports.

<u>How to use it right now:</u> Share the list with your school/district leaders to see what is already in place. Determine which screening tool best suits the needs of your school/district. Implement these screening procedures and assess/evaluate at least triennially.

II. **Steps to Conduct a Basic Pilot (Feasibility) Study in Your District to Screen for Behavioral Problems in Students (Appendix H)**

<u>What:</u> If a school and/or district is considering full-blown MTSS implementation, there is no better way to tackle it than by running a pilot program on a very small scale. This is excellent practice and will help you and your school prepare for a broader implementation. It allows for mistakes but not "nail-in-the-coffin" mistakes. Sometimes we just have to jump in and figure it out.

<u>Why:</u> Sooner or later, you and your district school will have to take the leap. Why not do it now, get it over with, and learn more about implementing a new approach your own way? Books and resources are great, but applied practice holds the real answers to authentic success. Your situation will be different than most when

it comes to implementation, simply because there are so many variables across each of our schools/districts, from leadership to funding to personnel.

How to use it right now: Use Appendix H as a basic planning guide to implement a small-scale pilot study on MTSS implementation, data collection, and progress monitoring.

III. **Influence Tips From Robert Cialdini (Appendix I)**

What: Sales tips and tricks to get ideas pushed up on the priority lists of decision makers/consumers (i.e., principals, school board members, colleagues, etc.).

Why: School and/or district leadership is faced with multiple "high-priority" needs on a daily basis. Engaged school leaders are engulfed in the competing needs of faculty, staff, parents, and their own initiatives. In other words, "everyone thinks their baby is the cutest" and leaders are forced to prioritize each of these pressing needs. How do you get your ideas to rise to the top? How do you gain influence over decisions made by stakeholders and leadership? Salespeople have been answering these questions for a long time. Use some of their tricks of the trade to get your ideas to the top of the heap.

How to use it right now: Use the six principles of influence to guide you in the sales tips and tricks of implementing a broad school-based initiative like universal screening for behavioral and emotional problems.

Happy Kids
Don't Punch You
in the Face

The mind is its own place, and in itself can make a heaven of hell, a hell of heaven.

—John Milton (1667)

For a few years, I worked in an office located in an alternative high school. The office was in a hallway between two classrooms. I enjoyed this setting because I was able to interact with a broad range of students from all walks of life. The school served students with alternative schedules, as well as students in the school district's post–high school program. The post–high school program was a work-based learning program for students with disabilities where they could work on areas that engendered independence, job skills, and comfort navigating the community. While I occasionally interacted with the students, much of my time was spent writing reports in my office.

On one such occasion, I heard a series of troubling noises coming from the classroom down the hall. What started with a loud clank crescendoed into the most amazing combination of profanity and threats I have ever heard in my entire life. (Note: I grew up with three brothers, participated in competitive sports, and generally adore the use of well-orchestrated profanity, and I *still* couldn't believe my ears.) This strand was threatening, vulgar, and terrifying.

As the de facto "behavior specialist" for the school district, I am embarrassed to admit that I was tempted to just close my door and "disappear." Yet my curiosity and sense of duty persevered. I walked through a group of students who were scurrying out the door with expressions of fear, confusion, and disbelief on their faces. When I entered the classroom, I saw Samantha swinging a computer keyboard around her head like a lasso.

Samantha was a 21-year-old on the autism spectrum. She was there to attend the school's post–high school program, and something had provoked her into what can only be described as a psychotic outburst. I later learned that Samantha lost control because she heard students in the classroom clapping. It's not an uncommon thing to hear in a public space, but for Samantha, clapping was an extreme trigger for aggression. But where did that aversion come from, and why did she react so fiercely to this particular trigger? Before we get there, let me tell you a little bit about Samantha.

She had attended school in that same district her entire life. At some point in her early academic experiences (which were very difficult based on her limited language ability, heightened anxiety, and impaired understanding of social situations), she had developed an acute aversion to clapping. Her parents had included her in multiple neurological studies and behavioral therapies to determine why her response to clapping was so volatile. Sixteen years later, very little understanding had been achieved and Samantha's response had become entrenched and essentially automatic.

Because Samantha was growing up with the same peer group year after year, her peers were aware of this phenomenon. While most students respected the boundaries and admonitions to avoid clapping around her, not all students were so kind. In fact, some students were downright mean and horribly insensitive to Samantha. Knowing that she would become extremely upset and engage in bewildering fits, some of these insensitive students would purposefully clap their hands to enrage her. This cruel behavior made Samantha's outbursts much worse, because she knew exactly what they were doing. So Samantha had this double whammy of a problem at school: accidental clapping and intentional clapping. Neither was good, but the latter really hurt and enraged her.

You can imagine how awful many years of Samantha's life at school were. I often wondered what it must have felt like for Samantha to attend school avoiding assemblies, celebrations, and any unsupervised group of children for fear of clapping and her subsequent loss of control.

When I entered the room, Samantha was seething. She did not have much faith in her peers' respect for the zero-clapping rule and she wanted to visit the full measure of her wrath upon those responsible. She was standing close to the entrance of the computer lab, and I knew that her classroom was only a few feet away. I gave Samantha a firm command to come with me next door to calm down. I reassured her that we would find out who had clapped and why. Samantha tentatively complied by stomping into her classroom, where she paced back and forth like a Bengal tiger in captivity. She belted out a few more incredibly profane and vulgar epithets that included the words *skull*, *sockets*, and *holes*, in no particular order.

FINDING A HAPPY PLACE

If ever there was an embodiment of the opposite of "happy," it would look like Samantha on that day. Rage and despair had completely consumed her, and she was inconsolable. Cases like Samantha's (along with every other tough case I have worked on) have forced me into some serious introspection about how our school systems are not always equipped or designed to help the students with whom I spend most of my time. Take Samantha's situation as an example. School was a nightmare for her, and she never got the kind of support she needed. When she was in school 16 years ago, academic leadership didn't have the awareness of and advocacy for autism that there is today (and even today the understanding related to students with exceptionalities manages to be only about an inch deep and a mile wide). In other words, I get angry. I get fed up with the way kids with special needs are mistreated or even omitted from the discussion about what we are attempting to accomplish in education. Even when fed up, I have been trained to be a good soldier and continue to educate school teams about the needs of students like Samantha. I know to dutifully conduct functional behavioral assessments and draft behavior intervention plans to help students like Samantha succeed and overcome obstacles. Yet every once in a while, to combat my frustrations, I scour existing research and philosophies seeking other means to solutions.

One of my original forays down this rabbit hole led me to revisit the ideas and roots of Positive Psychology. Most of my training in graduate school focused on psychological assessment and Applied Behavior Analysis, so when my coursework did cover Positive Psychology in counseling and mental health, it was still a new approach. However, when I revisited these concepts after some real-life practice in the trenches, it was as if they had a renewed sense of relevance—a bit shinier and a bit more attractive. After diving in again, I became utterly convinced that I had found the perfect theoretical avenue for my personality and my professional acumen. I had started the search fairly dissatisfied with Samantha's circumstances, but what I found made me more hopeful than ever. I was no longer jaded; I was happy.

GETTING OUR HAPPY BACK:
THE ROOTS OF POSITIVE PSYCHOLOGY

Far be it from me to provide you the introduction to Positive Psychology when the fathers of Positive Psychology, Martin Seligman and Mihaly Csikszentmihalyi, did such a fantastic job back in the new millennium. Below is an excerpt from their article "Positive Psychology: An Introduction" in January 2000:

> Entering a new millennium, Americans face a historical choice. Left alone on the pinnacle of economic and political leadership, the United States can continue to increase its material wealth while ignoring the human needs of its people and those of the rest of the planet. Such a course is likely to lead to increasing selfishness, to alienation between the more and the less fortunate, and eventually to chaos and despair. At this juncture, the social and behavioral sciences can play an enormously important role. They can articulate a vision of the good life that is empirically sound while being understandable and attractive. They can show what actions lead to well-being, to positive individuals, and to thriving communities. (p. 5)

Seligman and Csikszentmihalyi were basically saying that at the turn of the century, the United States stood at the precipice of deciding to invest in materials or human beings. (I'll let you come to your own conclusions about which path the United States chose and whether we're closer to chaos and despair or happiness and fulfillment.)

The article went on to identify a serious flaw in the practice of psychology that nobody was really prepared for. Essentially, the article identified (very accurately) that the work of psychology since World War II was mostly a science of healing. It had concentrated on repairing damage within a disease model of human functioning. This model defines mental health as only something to fix, not something to celebrate. Such a narrow emphasis on things that were not working had completely neglected the things that *were* working for human beings. It is almost silly and embarrassing that for so many years the discipline of psychology kinda missed the mark. As the authors stated, "the aim of positive psychology is to begin to catalyze a change in the focus of psychology from preoccupation only with repairing the worst things in life to also building positive qualities" (Seligman & Csikszentmihalyi, 2000, p. 5).

Seligman sums up what we all should be doing in education quite succinctly here: "Raising children, I realized, is vastly more than fixing what is wrong with them. It is about identifying and nurturing their strongest qualities, what they own and are best at, and helping them find niches in which they can best live out these strengths" (Seligman & Csikszentmihalyi, 2000, p. 10).

From this realization, Seligman has carved out a modern-day discipline in psychology that focuses primarily on three domains: (1) experiences (what makes one moment "better" than the next), (2) positive personalities (self-organizing, self-directed, and adaptive), and (3) social context (the role of people and experiences embedded into their social circles).

I was all in. I was hungry for more information from this gold mine. Particularly, I was hungry for applications of Positive Psychology in the school setting. Then it happened: I came across an article in a school psychology journal. Like most educators who find their way into the world of peer-revised journals, I tend to skim the articles that have piqued my interest until I reach the results section. That's where the application is, right? On this occasion, however, I was hooked. The abstract promised a theory so tantalizing, I couldn't help reading on. As I plowed through the article, I was amazed how salient the findings were to my individual struggles within the system.

The article is called "Reducing the Gap Between Research and Practice in School Psychology," by Thomas Kehle and Melissa Bray (2005). Both Kehle and Bray currently work at the University of Connecticut in the Educational Psychology Department, and if I ever get the chance to meet them, drinks are on me. Despite the fairly quotidian title, finding this article was my equivalent to discovering plutonium. It opened the doors to what would become the DNA of how I began conceptualizing my role working with children in the school setting.

While it was the abstract that grabbed my attention, the opening paragraph doubled down. See for yourself: "Despite sustained criticism of school psychological practices devoid of scientific bases, many still enjoy widespread popularity. The allegiance to these practices is at least partially caused by the practitioner's over-reliance on the medical model, intuition, tradition, and the belief in the righteousness of legislation" (Kehle & Bray, 2005, p. 577). Beautiful, right?

This one sentence managed to encapsulate everything I had experienced over the span of my career: We (school-based practitioners) had been aligned to inappropriate (e.g., medical models), archaic (e.g., intuition, tradition), and silly (e.g., legislative) practices for far too long. The article proceeded to tear down the banality of the legislative process and its negative influence on school policies while calling out the misuse of the medical model (observation and diagnostic testing) in school psychology.

As if these criticisms weren't enough to shake up current practices in our schools, Kehle and Bray identified the crux of the problems I had been experiencing up to that point in my career: There was (is) no unifying theory of education. Can you imagine the progress (or lack thereof) of the physical sciences if our scientific forbears refused to agree on the existence of gravity? It is ridiculous that in modern society there is no unifying theory regarding the proper way to educate and help our children succeed . . . or is there?

Kehle and Bray thoughtfully introduced a theory that encompasses ideas that are both old and new. The theory is old because we have wanted the same thing for our children since the dawn of the middle class (you know, the first time in history when humans actually had time to pay attention to children). The theory is new because we have barely scratched the surface of how to help our children find happiness and fulfillment. Fortunately, Kehle and Bray have done enough front-loading for each of us as school practitioners to start understanding this potential unifying theory. Kehle and Bray call this RICH theory, and it represents their attempt to identify the tenable components that everyone needs to be objectively happy: resources, intimacy, competence, and health (Kehle, 1989, 1999; Kehle & Bray, 2004; Kehle, Clark, & Jenson, 1993).

THE FOUR PILLARS OF HAPPINESS

The RICH theory (Kehle, 1989, 1999; Kehle & Barclay, 1979; Kehle, Bray, Chafouleas, & McLoughlin, 2002; Kehle et al., 1993) defines psychological health as being synonymous with happiness. According to Kehle and Bray, happiness has four characteristics, which I like to think of as pillars, or the structures that sustain happiness. These characteristics are interrelated to the extent that they incorporate one another in their definitions. Kehle and Bray (2005) note: "On the surface, resources, intimacy, competence, and health do not appear to be related; however, they are highly interrelated to the degree that they can be considered synonymous with each other" (p. 581).

What that means is that each of these pillars contributes to a state of general well-being for each of us and the children with whom we work. If we were to remove one of these pillars, we would be less happy, and so on to the point that if we were just talking about our health—we would not be too happy at all. Happiness is built on the following pillars.

Resources

Access to resources is a big deal for adults and kids. The ability to navigate one's environment in an independent and meaningful way cannot be overstated. Think for a moment how you felt when you learned to ride a bike for the first time or when you received your driver's license. That sense of freedom and autonomy was powerful; it continues to be powerful. Conversely, think of a time when your freedom and/or autonomy was taken away or "micromanaged." Take a moment to compare and contrast those feelings. We know how much we dislike having someone breathe down our necks and look over our shoulders; kids don't like it either. We have to try stuff on our own and get some feedback from our environment. We have to screw up, and we have to find success. It's the same with kids. These types of environmental feedback loops help all of us know that we exist. They help us understand that we count for something—that we make a difference and that our existence is relevant.

I have facilitated and conducted hundreds of psychological assessments over the past decade. As a psychologist, I can't help enjoying certain assessments and what they attempt to measure in children. A common metric I have found to be extremely valuable measures an individual's self-rated "locus of control" or "sense of inadequacy." These identifiers typically quantify the individual's feeling of importance or sense of environmental significance. In other words, they help the individual realize they are part of the fabric of existence. Can you imagine the feeling of having zero impact on your environment? Or the feeling of moving through life like a ghost? It is a feeling many kids deal with on a regular basis, and there are a variety of factors that contribute to this. One of the factors I personally have seen over the years is that some children become so controlled and micromanaged, they feel they have no viable meaning in their environments. This has an extremely negative impact on a child's sense of self-worth, and it's especially common among children struggling with behavior difficulties. Most of our approaches take punitive stances, reducing the child's independence by placing a one-on-one behavioral aide in the classroom or restricting access to common areas, and so on. These approaches end up limiting the child's access to resources, and their implementation effectively dismantles one of the pillars of happiness (Giangreco, Edelman, Luiselli, & MacFarland, 1999; Marks, Schrader, & Levine, 1999). We all know that we ought to be in the business of building pillars of happiness, not knocking them down.

Intimacy

When I began training multiple school districts in 2007 on integrating RICH Theory into practical behavior management strategies, I would joke by saying "Can you imagine standing in front of a school board or our state legislators and claiming that our kids need more intimacy training in schools?" I'm not sure if it even qualifies as a joke, but I could always rely on that comment to get laughs. Why? Why is it so funny to think of a school board or some legislator responding to teaching intimacy in schools?

My hunch is that concepts like intimacy and relationships have been so tainted by political discourse over the past century that they can no longer be discussed reasonably by anyone holding a political office. My hunch is that our modern legislative bodies have no real idea about what it takes to educate our youth. My hunch is that Kehle and Bray (2005) nailed it when they observed,

> *It is highly doubtful that legislation will alter children's achievement to any appreciable and enduring extent and the consequences for not doing so under such Draconian methods are grim not only for the professional administration and teaching staff, but for all of those involved in public education including the students the laws were intentionally designed to help.* (p. 578)

While political and legislative bodies may not get the joke, the importance of navigating intimate relationships as central to human happiness comes as no surprise to the rest of us. In Bertrand Russell's (1930) seminal work, *The Conquest of Happiness*, Russell claimed, "Companionship and cooperation are essential elements in the happiness of the average man" (p. 78). Why? Why are relationships so important to happiness? Kehle and Bray (2005) suggest that intimacy is not just the romantic intimacy shared between partners but also friendship. Intimacy involves empathy and the appreciation and enjoyment of a friend's company. We are not designed to be islands. We are happier together, in pairs, in small groups, and in families.

As a doctoral student at the University of Utah, I studied teaching social skills to children on the autism spectrum as well as children struggling with externalizing behavior disorders. I was stunned by how critical navigating social environments was (and is) for children. Social exchanges drive both language and cognitive development, and children who struggle with complex neurodevelopmental disorders along with deficits in social skills have higher rates of depression, anxiety, and agitation than their typically developing peers (Bellini, 2006; La Greca & Lopez, 1998; Tantam, 2000; Welsh, Park, Widaman, & O'Neil, 2001).

Children identified as "socially isolated" have been found to be at significant risk of poor adult health compared with non-isolated children. The association was independent of other well-established childhood risk factors for poor adult health (low childhood socioeconomic status, low childhood IQ, childhood obesity), was not accounted for by health-damaging behaviors (lack of exercise, smoking, alcohol abuse), and was not attributable to great exposure to stressful life events (Caspi & Moffit, 2006). In other words, just being lonely as a child is a serious health-risk factor.

Thus, there are some very real and very prescient arguments for teaching intimacy in our schools. A decade has passed since I began joking about pitching intimacy training to school boards and legislators. Recently, the laughs have been followed by some serious introspection, and I'm happy to say that some motivated educators are taking intimacy instruction, relationship building, and social skills back to their schools. What we are discovering is that, due to the already high demand on schools' time and resources, there is not enough time for successful implementation. My dissertation research investigated what it actually took to have an educator teach social skills in the school setting. The results? It takes time, follow-up, and repetition throughout the school year to make any meaningful difference (Springer, 2012). Is the time worth it? You bet. It's worth it for both adults and kids. Developing relationships is critical work. We know this, yet we very rarely do anything about it. This is a pillar that would benefit all of us, our kids included.

Competence

I have been working in public education settings for a long time. I am very aware of the weaknesses that exist in our school systems. They are real and make schools woefully similar to the highways in my home state: perennially under construction and reform. This is neither good nor bad; it's just not always the smoothest ride, that's all.

Despite the bumps in the road, there are a lot of really great educators and leaders in public schools working diligently to help kids succeed in academic areas. In fact, I would argue that out of all these pillars of happiness, our school systems do a pretty darn good job with this one. I go to work every day astounded by what teachers are able to accomplish in classrooms full of increasingly diverse student populations and heterogeneous learners. On a daily basis, I witness teachers helping students achieve competence in at least one (if not all) of the primary areas of math, language arts, and science. Kehle and Bray (2005) have concluded that competence in at least one of these areas is all we really need to hold up this pillar of happiness. We just need to be competent, not experts. Interestingly, competence in academic areas is not the only thing we should be working toward. What other areas should we be competent in when we leave school and look for a career?

The National Association of Colleges and Employers (NACE) is a nonprofit group from Pennsylvania that links career placement offices with employers. NACE (2015) ran a survey from mid-August through early October where it asked business and hiring managers what skills they plan to prioritize when they recruit from the class of 2015 at colleges and graduate schools. The top five responses from 260 employers, including companies like Chevron and IBM, were (1) ability to work in a team structure; (2) ability to make decisions and solve problems; (3) ability to communicate verbally with people inside and outside an organization; (4) ability to plan, organize, and prioritize work; and (5) ability to obtain and process information.

There's no question that we want our children to become competent in the core areas of instruction (language arts, math calculation/reasoning, scientific analysis, etc.) during their time spent at school. However, consider a student who may struggle in one of those core areas. Based on the results of the NACE survey, that student still may be very marketable if they are competent in any of the top five employable skills. In other words, becoming competent does not mean being an expert, nor is it reserved for purely academic pursuits. Competence is a pillar of happiness because competence is realistic and empowering. Each of us can reach competence in at least one thing. This isn't "lowering the bar" or anything; it is simply acknowledging that happiness is not necessarily associated with mastery and/or expertise.

Health

It should come as no surprise that we are happy when we are healthy. When we become less healthy, we become less happy. When our health or the health of loved ones declines rapidly, our happiness declines rapidly (Druss & Pincus, 2000). During times of medical or functional decline, hopelessness, depression, and suicide ideation often co-occur (Roose, Glassman, & Seidman, 2001) and may contribute to a cycle of distress and despair.

This is alarming considering the recent health statistics associated with school-age children (Ogden, Carroll, Kit, & Flegal, 2014). Children today are largely sedentary. Most children spend only 8 to 10 minutes per day on aerobic activity. What are kids doing when they're sitting around? You know exactly what they're doing: staring at screens. The Mayo Clinic has recently updated its informational website to include "screen time guidelines," in conjunction with the American Academy of Pediatrics. The guidelines state, "As your child grows, keep in mind that too much or poor quality screen time has been linked to: 1) obesity, 2) irregular sleep patterns, 3) behavioral problems, 4) loss of social skills, 5) violence, 6) less time for play" (Mayo Clinic Staff, 2016). In other words, there's not only a quantity but a quality dynamic to consider as parents and teachers use the screens available in modern-day school settings.

Combine the sedentary lifestyle with the precarious dietary habits of children and we get a recipe for poor health outcomes ranging from chronic constipation (Belsey, Greenfield, Candy, & Geraint, 2010) to type 2 diabetes (Dabelea et al., 2014), and everything in between. Health concerns like these inevitably contribute to the overall stress in a child's life. Anger, aggression, frustration, and poor impulse control occur for a variety of reasons; it is reasonable to conclude that some of the reasons are related to somatic discomfort. This pillar of happiness clearly requires more attention in our schools and should be investigated prior to making any big decisions affecting student behavior management.

THEORY TO PRACTICE IN THE SCHOOL SETTING

Although Kehle and Bray have identified what seems to be a pretty darn good unifying theory of education, the traction for this theory has not necessarily caught on. Of course, advancing theories into practice has never really been a strength of modern-day schools. These things take time, but I don't think they need to take much *more* time. Neither does Shannon Suldo. She is a psychologist from the University of South Florida and is the premier researcher when it comes to applying aspects of happiness research in schools. Her work has been continually published throughout the past decade and has helped guide practitioners in the importance of life satisfaction (aka subjective well-being, aka happiness). In 2006, Suldo and Huebner made a profound observation while studying happiness in adolescents: The absence of mental illness is not synonymous with the presence of mental health or considerable happiness. In other words, children with mental health concerns can actually be super happy, and children without mental health concerns can be dissatisfied and bummed out about life. These findings indicated that our previous efforts to understand and prevent mental illness may not be sufficient to identify and nurture optimal mental health.

Just so we're clear, I think I'd like to repeat that last finding: Our previous efforts to understand and prevent mental illness may not be sufficient to identify and nurture optimal mental health. Translation: Our practices for the past century are no longer sufficient to help children reach high-quality life satisfaction (which, after all, should be the unifying theory of everything when it comes to working with kids, right?).

These conclusions were consistent with the work from Diener and Seligman's (2002) study with adults. Suldo and Huebner's 2006 study was the first study of extremely high subjective well-being (happiness) in youths. You read that right: The first study to tackle happiness of students in the school setting didn't happen until 2006. We have just started to scratch the surface of how to help children reach fulfillment and happiness. Because this work is relatively new in the field of education, let's take some time to look at what has been done outside the field of education on these concepts of "extremely high life satisfaction" and "subjective well-being." Let's look at what Csikszentmihalyi calls the psychology of optimal experience, or flow.

GOT FLOW?

All right, I've geeked out on Positive Psychology enough, and hopefully I have presented a pretty strong case as to why and how we should apply its concepts to the school setting. Now I want to provide you with some background on a practical idea that will help you carry all this out—a Zen-like concept known as flow. It's a term coined by the Hungarian psychologist Mihaly Csikszentmihalyi to describe the feeling of an optimal experience that is tantamount to the feeling of happiness. Csikszentmihalyi has conducted research for a quarter century to provide each of us with a road map for how to find and experience flow. It is my belief (and the heart of this book and my practice) that the experience of flow not only replaces and prevents aggressive and/or dangerous behavior but leads kids to a happier life. This is the goal. This is the point. This is why we do what we do. Happy kids simply do not punch you in the face. On that note, Csikszentmihalyi (1991) states very deliberately:

> Happiness is not something that happens. It is not the result of good fortune or random chance. It is not something that money can buy or power can command. It does not depend on outside events, but, rather, on how we interpret them. Happiness, in fact, is a conduction that must be prepared for, cultivated, and defended privately by each person. People who learn to control inner experience will be able to determine the quality of their lives, which is as close as any of us can come to being happy. (p. 2)

There you have it. "People who learn to control inner experience will be able to determine the quality of their lives." Seem crazy? Seem impractical? Nonsense. Since this theory was published, it has inspired the creation of experimental school curricula, the training of business executives, and the design of leisure products and services. Flow is being used to generate ideas and practices in clinical psychotherapy, the rehabilitation of juvenile delinquents, the design of museum exhibits, and occupational therapy with individuals with disabilities (Csikszentmihalyi, 1991).

We're going to use it to help de-escalate aggressive outbursts from students like Trevor, Luis, Chrissie, and Samantha. We're going to use it to help prevent those outbursts. We're going to use it to respond to those outbursts. We're going to use it. Period. We can do this. You can do this. It's actually really fun, too!

HOW FLOW BECAME FLOW

Prior to jumping into the steps to achieving optimal experience or flow, it is worth understanding how Csikszentmihalyi came to his discoveries of flow and happiness. Back when he started his research, he used basic interviews and questionnaires with students on the college campus. While that was fine, Csikszentmihalyi's stroke of genius was the use of electronic pagers. (For those of you unfamiliar with pagers, they were basically the precursor to the cell phone. They were little electronic gadgets you could keep in a pocket or on your belt that could relay basic code, like numbers and letters. Medical doctors used them quite a bit in the late '80s and '90s to be on call for their patients and colleagues.)

Well, Csikszentmihalyi used these little gadgets in what he called the Experience Sampling Method. This method was brilliant because he and his team could aggregate and disaggregate a very large number of responses. Participants in his studies would wear the pager, and when prompted, they would journal how they felt and what they were thinking multiple times a day—at random. The responders expanded from students on college campuses to over a hundred thousand (and counting) cross sections of experiences from different parts of the world. This level of data collection is basically unheard of in the social sciences. These data were what Csikszentmihalyi built his theory on—and the foundation is only getting stronger.

THE PATH TO FLOW

If we conceptualize flow and happiness as our destination, Csikszentmihalyi has provided a map of eight major landmarks and trails. I have applied this map in my practice to draft behavior plans and even individualized education plans. Table 2 provides an overview of each of these steps.

Table 2 The Eight Major Steps to Achieving Flow or Optimal Experience

Step		Definition	Why It Leads to Flow
1	A challenging activity that requires skill	An activity that is goal-directed and bounded by rules	Turns out, there has to be something to do—and it has to be challenging. (This can be an assignment, a conversation, anything.)
2	Ability to concentrate on what one is doing	The merging of action and awareness. This occurs when all a person's relevant skills are needed to cope with the challenges of the situation.	When kids become very involved in what they are doing, the activity becomes spontaneous, almost automatic.
3	A clear (understood) goal	A clear, unarguable outcome that will be easy to conclude if it has been attained or not	Unless a child learns to set goals and to recognize and gauge feedback, they will not enjoy them.
4	Immediate feedback	Regular information after every attempt toward completion of a task	The kind of feedback we work toward is often unimportant. The key ingredient is that it indicates success or an approximation of success.
5	Deep but effortless involvement that removes worries and frustrations from daily life (I think this is also called "fun.")	The task is designed to be so engaging as to engulf the attention of the child.	The task essentially distracts the child from their worries and fears.
6	Sense of control and choice	The ability, in the midst of a challenging task or situation, to make a choice that minimizes failure	What kids enjoy is not the sense of being in control but the sense of exercising control in difficult situations.
7	Sense of improvement and success after completing the task	The process by which we gauge our movement through the task at hand	Being able to forget temporarily who we are seems to be very enjoyable. When not preoccupied with ourselves, we actually have a chance to expand the concept of who we are.
8	An altered sense of the duration of time	We don't pay attention to passing time.	Although it seems likely that losing track of time is not the major element of enjoyment, freedom from the tyranny of time does add to the exhilaration we feel.

Adapted from Csikszentmihalyi (1991).

Table 2 provides a pretty straightforward road map. I think there are real-life applications for these steps (and I'll provide those real-life applications in the appendices), but we should consider why they work, right? As confident as I am in these steps, I think it is also important that we, as practitioners, have a deeper understanding of them so we can apply the concepts more universally in our approaches. In other words, I think we can become Betty Crocker as opposed to limiting ourselves to the recipes she's printed on the back of her products. Figure 3 is your first step to becoming the Betty Crocker of happiness—able to whip up rich, sugar-frosted happiness in a jiffy!

Csikszentmihalyi has done plenty of brilliant things for the world of psychology, but this flow chart is at the top of my list (see Figure 3). The beauty is in the conceptualization. What Csikszentmihalyi found was that there are two primary variables that must always be present for flow—or happiness—to exist. The first variable is *challenge*. As you can see, challenge is on the y-axis, with values ranging from low to high. The second variable is *skill*. *Skill* has been placed on the x-axis with values ranging from low to high as well. The interaction between these two variables results in very concrete and identifiable moods or feelings.

As an educational practitioner, consider where we do our best work with students on the Flow Chart in Figure 3. If I were to guess, we would want students to fall somewhere between the lower and upper right side of the chart (i.e., relaxation, feeling in control, arousal).

Figure 3 Csikszentmihalyi's Flow Chart

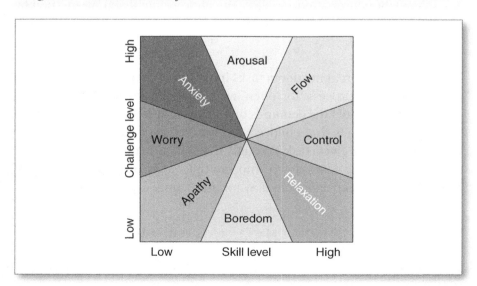

Source: user: Oliverbeatson / Wikimedia Commons / Public Domain

For students to fall in the conditions most conducive to learning, Figure 3 indicates that at a very minimum, the skills of the students must be high. Therefore, most of our efforts should emphasize skill development. What skills? All the skills necessary to meet the challenges we have whipped up in a lesson, an activity, or within a curriculum. There are many methods by which we can identify the skills required for students (in fact, many educators understand this concept of prerequisites very well). My background and training refer to this process as task analysis. Szidon and Franzone (2009) present the following steps involved in breaking down a skill into smaller, more manageable components:

1. Teachers/practitioners identify the target skill they want to teach the students.

2. Teachers/practitioners determine whether the students have the required prerequisite skills needed to learn the task.

3. Teachers/practitioners define the necessary materials needed to teach the task.

4. Students break the skill into components by breaking the skills down themselves and recording each step or by observing another person (in real time or via video recording) complete the activity and recording that person's steps.

5. Teachers/practitioners confirm that each component consists of a discrete skill.

6. Teachers/practitioners select the appropriate teaching method by matching the method to the students' particular strengths and weaknesses.

The value in breaking down tasks into discrete steps is that it can help facilitate the flow process. Too often, we go through the motions, ignoring just how complicated the demands of any given task may be. The problem with this passivity is that children can lose sense of the meaningfulness and purpose of a given task through the constant negotiating for good behavior. Breaking tasks down into multiple steps helps us direct them toward the road map ending in flow (or an optimal experience).

THE LOW-SKILL/HIGH-CHALLENGE DILEMMA

It seems that the longer I work in the profession, the more students I work with who are on the autism spectrum. I love it. Autism has always been fascinating to me, and I enjoy working with children and families affected by it. (I used to wonder why I liked it, until I read about flow; now I totally get it. It is the matchup of the challenges and skills!) So, as it turns out, autism is a complex neurodevelopmental disorder affecting everything from attention to language to social skills to sensory processing to mood regulation. One of the hallmark characteristics of autism is the lack of (or impaired) social skills. Social skills are best defined as the actions we take to initiate, respond to, and maintain social relationships.

So referencing Figure 3, a child with autism most likely has low social skills, and it really isn't their fault. What do you imagine the challenges (both in and out of our control) are for communicating socially in the school setting? High or low? Of course the social challenges of school are incredibly high. So according to Figure 3, what mood or feeling is a student on the autism spectrum experiencing prior to even sitting down in class? Anxiety—and a ton of it. That means before we even get a chance to give an assignment or a direction to a student on the autism spectrum, there is a high probability that the student is experiencing serious levels of elevated anxiety.

Imagine for a moment what that must feel like, to have a general layer of anxiety and then constantly be challenged by a task or situation. If it is difficult to imagine, I will share with you a scenario I provide to parents and teachers when I have diagnosed or identified autism in a child for the first time. I enlist this scenario to help parents and teachers understand how difficult a day at school can be for someone on the autism spectrum.

The Chinese Subway Scenario

Imagine you are traveling abroad in China, by yourself, and you're hungry. You find yourself in a subway, hundreds of feet beneath the surface. There are no landmarks and only two trains. One of the trains will head to the city center, where you will certainly find some food. The other train will head to the country, where it is much less likely you will find some food.

You do not understand any Chinese, and the subway is super crowded. As you attempt to ask questions, most of the folks in the subway are too busy to help you or listen to you, and none of them actually understands you. When they do speak to you, their volume and tone kind of make you feel like they are angry at you. All you really want is some food and some directions. How do you feel in that moment? How prepared would you be to complete a math assignment in that moment?

You would most likely be experiencing anxiety combined with stress and an empty stomach. That state is not optimal for learning; it's not optimal for anything positive, for that matter. Yet students on the autism spectrum enter school every day in a mental state a lot like that. Prolonged exposure to that amount of psychological discomfort will most likely result in frustration, anger, agitation, and aggression. It has nothing to do with IQ or personality; it is the dynamic interplay between the challenges and their skills. The challenges simply do not match their skill sets.

SO WHAT?

We need a unifying theory of education. We need to start garnering some consensus on what our independent variables (what we teach) and our dependent variables (what kids learn) should be. We need this because without consensus, we will continually be spinning our wheels and getting nowhere. Kehle and Bray posited that the RICH Theory could serve as this unifying theory of education. The independent variable in this theory involves teaching children how to access resources, maintain and enrich intimacy, become competent in at least one area, and live a healthy lifestyle. The theory's dependent variable is happiness and fulfillment for students.

We need to understand why focusing on RICH Theory and happiness is important for children. Seligman, Csikszentmihalyi, and Suldo (backed up by vast teams of researchers) have built a strong case for why happiness is not just a goal in life but *the* goal in life. We need to understand that kids can operate and focus on only one mood at a time. If they are exposed to skills and challenges that bring them happiness instead of frustration and anger, they will be less likely to act out aggressively.

We need to understand that there are real, reproducible steps for becoming happy in life and that there are multiple ways to achieve happiness based on human diversity. We need to work diligently as educators to build these steps and maps for our students. While these strategies should be made available and prioritized for every student, I believe they should be the top priority for students struggling with behavioral and emotional problems.

We also need to understand the dynamic interplay between the individual and social challenges children face and the skills they possess. I believe understanding of this dynamic comes through both formal (norm-referenced, standardized) and informal assessment (building rapport and relationships with kids, getting to know them). In keeping with my love of putting theory into practice, the following tools section is going to set you up not only in the basics of understanding Positive Psychology but also in the application of flow in the school setting.

READY-TO-USE TOOLS (CHAPTER 4)

I. **Applications of RICH Theory to IEP Goals and BIP Goals (Appendix J)**

<u>What:</u> Applying a theoretical construct to practice can be tricky. This tool will help you identify aspects of the RICH Theory built within individualized education plans (IEPs) and behavior intervention plans (BIPs) commonly used throughout special education.

<u>Why:</u> This entire book and approach is about applying research and theory to practice. Start bringing a little happiness and joy to the students exhibiting aggressive behavior.

<u>How to use it right now:</u> Share and chew on Appendix J with colleagues who are facing the task of drafting IEP goals and BIP goals for students. Measure progress and whether or not aggressive behavior increases or decreases.

Principles of
Applied Behavior
Analysis

Never trust to general impressions, my boy, but concentrate yourself upon details.

—Arthur Conan Doyle, *The Adventures of Sherlock Holmes* (1892)

After an introductory year as an assistant, I became a lead autism specialist at one of the premier Applied Behavior Analysis (ABA)–based programs for children in Utah. In my eagerness, I worked diligently to try to figure out this ABA business. I had been taught how to arrange consequences to increase/decrease behavior, build discrete trial programs, direct backward/forward chaining, shape behavior—you name it! I felt as though I had transcended to a new level of understanding. I felt as though problem behaviors trembled at the very sound of my name! Until I met Tino.

One April morning, I was called to the front office for assistance. When I arrived, it looked like the scene of a burglary. Claire, our lovely administrative assistant, was backed up against the wall as if standing on the edge of a tall building.

Claire pointed silently toward my right shoulder. When I turned to look, there stood Tino with a ripped shirt and one shoe off, looking like he had just been rescued from a desert island.

Tino was only 8 years old, short in stature, with eyes as wild as any you have ever seen. Claire had called me down because his parents were busy in the intake office with our social worker. Claire was unprepared for Tino's panicked separation from his parents, which had resulted in tornadoesque destruction of the front office. Once again, I performed my ill-advised crouch-'n'-smile maneuver to introduce myself to Tino. Tino promptly spit in my face and then ran for the door.

I quickly wiped the spit from my cheek and asked Tino if he was looking for his mom or dad. He looked at me cautiously and made a "yeh" sound. I reached out my hand, signaling he could hold it, and he obliged. We exited the front office, and I began distracting Tino from the absence of his parents by walking with him down the hall and allowing him to push buttons on the elevator and the drinking fountain.

After intake was completed (and the office repaired), the administration decided to place Tino in my classroom. I was excited for the challenge and felt that my classroom was ready. We had been working all year, and most of our class was operating like a well-oiled machine. Tino was only slightly verbal, and our assessment (plus parent request) suggested that Tino participate in an attending program. Attending programs are activities designed through a process known as discrete trial. Discrete trials sequentially build and chain behaviors associated with sitting still and following directions. In other words, Tino was working on sitting, listening, and chilling out a little.

At any given time, we had three or four students working on some level of an attending program. We placed Tino on a pretty intensive daily regimen working with peers in small groups as well as having some one-on-one time with staff.

On a fateful spring afternoon, Tino was working with one of our paraprofessionals, Jody. Jody had Tino and three other students in front of her in a kind of half circle. Tino was on her left side between two peers. In what must have been some sort of lightning-fast impulse, Tino lunged forward and bit into Jody's breast.

We labeled her scream that day "The Shriek Heard 'Round the World." Poor Jody was patient zero in the soon-to-be epidemic of Tino breast bites. After that scream, no breast near Tino was safe. Prior to that event, Tino had never exhibited breast-biting behavior. The data we had collected at that point were pretty clear: The scream accidentally reinforced Tino's breast-biting behavior and he was generalizing that behavior beyond the school setting. Tino began biting his mother's breasts as well as those of complete strangers at the supermarket. It was bad.

With only a year and half under my belt in ABA-based approaches, I suddenly realized how inexperienced I was. I had no solid answers for Tino's breast-biting behavior. I had to hit the books again and really study how to reverse a dangerous behavior trend. As fond as I am of Positive Psychology and the concepts of flow, in this instance, nobody wanted to hear about why Tino was unhappy; they just wanted him to stop biting breasts. It is for situations like this that we need tools and strategies. We need ABA and the roll-up-your-sleeves ethics associated with behavior modification.

THE ROOTS OF ABA

Ivan Pavlov and Edward Thorndike essentially created what we now know as ABA through their experiments and research in classical conditioning (Pavlov's dogs) and association (Thorndike's cats). Pavlov and Thorndike were undoubtedly students of the tabula rasa (Team Nurture) philosophy of John Locke. Their work was galvanized into behaviorism by John Watson, who rejected concepts like the mind, instinct, thought, and emotion. While Watson's contributions lost some luster after he infamously traumatized a baby with white rats, it was researchers like B. F. Skinner who brought principles of ABA to the forefront.

Skinner essentially discovered that there was much more to "conditioning" than simply stimulus–response. He coined this discovery *instrumental conditioning* or *operant conditioning*. Skinner found through a variety of studies that behavior could be shaped by manipulating consequences. His studies burgeoned into full-blown applications in the 1960s. It seemed the tenets that drove animal behavior could also drive human behavior. These tenets have been rigorously studied since the late '60s, resulting in a mountain of evidence supporting their use (Howard, Sparkman, Cohen, Green, & Stanislaw, 2005).

THE ABCS OF ABA

The scope of this chapter is not to incorporate every single concept, procedure, and program associated with ABA. The scope of this chapter is to provide some accessible strategies to help manage aggressive behavior. If you would like to know more about the practical use of ABA in the school setting, I highly recommend the text by O'Neill, Albin, Storey, Horner, and Sprague (2015) called *Functional Assessment and Program Development for Problem Behavior: A Practical Handbook*, as well as the text from Alberto and Troutman (2012) called *Applied Behavior Analysis for Teachers*.

There are plenty of board-certified and licensed professionals trained in ABA, and some of them might even be working in your school. Such professionals are a great resource and will undoubtedly possess the training necessary to help you out. What I don't want you to think is that ABA is exclusively reserved for those with board certifications and/or professional licenses. In fact, there are some very basic tenets of ABA that should be used by everyone on the school team, regardless of their background. These tenets are referred to as the ABCs of ABA. The acronym helps practitioners remember the steps to an incredibly effective problem-solving method when confronted with problem behavior.

The A stands for *antecedent*, the B stands for *behavior*, and the C stands for *consequence*. More specifically, the acronym can represent the expanded terms (1) antecedent management, (2) behavior identification, and (3) consequence management. Essentially, these steps create a formula that helps us address what is contributing to a behavior and how to change that behavior.

The ABC framework is designed to help us build a case (like Sherlock Holmes or Batman would) regarding the function or purpose of a behavior. Once we have followed these steps, we can come up with a strategy to combat the negative behaviors we have seen by changing some things in the environment, teaching new skills, and arranging consequences (for good and bad behavior).

Most of the time, team members or parents will contact us about the B (behavior) first. In the case of Tino, the observed behavior was glaringly obvious—breast biting. Instead of building our case from there, ABA dictates that we follow the ABC sequence to properly address the problem. So with the breast biting, we had to start with A (antecedent).

Antecedent Management

The most basic and essential components of this step are documenting the time of day, place, people involved, and activity right before the behavior occurred. Once we have documented these areas, I like to use the following questions to help plan preventive and responsive strategies: What events led up to the behavior? What in the environment contributed to the onset of the behavior? Is there anything in the environment we can change to prevent the behavior from happening again?

Documenting the time, place, people, and activity, as well as answering the questions, forms the first step in the ABC sequence. The answers to these questions can help us brainstorm ideas to manage the environment in a way that prevents the behavior from happening again. The steps for Tino are provided in Table 3.

Based on the responses provided in this step, it sounds like we could attempt to modify the proximity of Tino to staff, modify seating arrangements, change the size of the group, wear protective fabric, and keep Tino

Table 3   Antecedent Management Steps

Antecedent Management Steps	Responses
Time of day	9:47 a.m.
Place	Classroom
People involved	Tino and Jody
Activity	Small-group instruction (matching shapes and colors)
What events led up to the behavior?	Tino was sitting in a small group with three peers. Jody was attending to another student right before she was bitten.
What (if anything) in the environment contributed to the onset of the behavior	The proximity of Tino to Jody contributed to the onset. Jody was working with multiple students and could not see the bite coming. Jody and the team have to sit close to Tino, because if we don't keep him nearby, he can get up and run around.
Is there anything in the environment we can change to prevent the behavior from happening again?	We can modify the seating arrangements, modify our clothing to thicker/protective fabric, and keep Tino at arm's length until the behavior is extinguished.

at arm's length. We should also monitor to see if the behavior occurs in any sort of pattern (e.g., same time of day, with the same people, or during the same activity). Once we've completed this step, we need to keep it at the ready, because it will be included in the culminating steps of our behavior plan.

Now that we've successfully completed the *A* step in this process, we can move on to the *B* step. This step involves our defining the behaviors we want to see decrease (e.g., breast biting) and the behaviors we want to see increase (e.g., keeping teeth behind those lips).

Behavior Identification

While this step is fairly straightforward, it is important to be specific when identifying behaviors. Fortunately, the breast-biting example is pretty specific. In practice, just remember to avoid describing the behavior in vague terms. For instance, avoid describing a tantrum as "a tantrum." Break down the actions involved in a tantrum into specific parts, like stomping feet, screaming at a high volume, and waving hands.

The rationale behind being descriptive is that the more accurately we can identify the behaviors we want to see decrease (e.g., breast biting, hitting, kicking), the more accurately we can identify the behaviors we want to see increase (e.g., keeping teeth behind lips, keeping hands in pockets, and keeping feet on the ground). Once we have a clear idea of positive behaviors we want to see increase, we can teach and reinforce them.

By ramping up our efforts to instruct and reward the new target replacement behavior, we give the child fewer and fewer opportunities to engage in the negative behavior.

At the end of the day, it is a race. The negative behavior and the target replacement behavior are in constant competition. No matter what, there can be only one winner. Human beings can't engage in two incompatible behaviors at the same time. For Tino, it was impossible for him to bite a breast *and* keep his teeth behind his lips. So either breast biting or keeping teeth behind the lips was going to win.

Obviously, we can't leave the outcome of this race up to chance. Simply identifying a positive replacement behavior is not enough. We need to rig the race. We need to teach the positive replacement behavior and reinforce that behavior at a significantly higher rate than we administer consequences for the negative behavior. (Appendix K provides a fun, field-tested worksheet for conducting "The Replacement Behavior Race." This worksheet walks you through all the steps necessary to "rig the race" in favor of the competing positive replacement behavior.)

Consequence Management

The last step in the ABC sequence is managing the consequences for both good and bad behaviors. Prior to managing consequences, it is worth understanding what the heck consequences are. A lot of folks think consequences exist only for bad behavior. In ABA, that is not the case. In ABA, consequences never sleep. In other words, every single action has a consequence, whether we like it or not. Some of these consequences increase the likelihood of the action taking place again; some of them decrease the likelihood of the action recurring. The way we manage these consequences can dictate the duration, frequency, and intensity of almost any behavior.

In this final step, we have to take a basic inventory of what we have accomplished with the previous two steps. First, we must tweak some minor aspects of the environment to help prevent or minimize the probability of a negative behavior taking place. Second, we must identify behaviors we would like to decrease and behaviors we would like to increase. Third, we must make an itemized list of the consequences we will deliver to manage both the bad behavior (behavior to decrease) and the good behavior (behavior to increase). Let's continue to use Tino and the breast-biting dilemma to work through this step.

What should Tino's consequence be when he bit a breast? Without any consequence management, the unconditioned response or consequence had been a scream, a shriek, or a wince (and on one or two occasions, a curse word). These consequences were almost impossible to prevent when Tino engaged in the behavior. Obviously, breasts are incredibly sensitive, and the automatic response of most every victim to that excruciating pain was an audible cry. Still we had to control for this consequence. We were not certain about the function of Tino's behavior, but we did not want Tino to be able to engage in the behavior and then get out of work or get more attention. So if and when Tino bit a staff member, she would leave immediately, cry it out, and come back when she was ready. We each agreed to use a code word to help cover the injured staff member's group or activity. So any time a staff member left abruptly, we would say "snowball" and the nearest (or most available) staff member would take over Tino's session.

This consequence helped us control for any unintended reinforcement of Tino's behavior (just in case he was biting either to get out of work and/or to get the attention of the staff member). Even with our snowball procedure, Tino was observed to engage in the behavior; so we needed another consequence. Our first choice was boredom. As soon as Tino bit and someone rotated to his session, the new person would do their best to remain emotionally neutral and would give Tino two phonebooks taped together to hold. Tino would inevitably push the phonebooks off his lap, but we would simply give them back to him. (This was much easier than trying to fend off more bites or slaps or kicks.) After one or two phonebook holds, we would go right back to the work session routines.

On the flip side, we created a consequence for when Tino kept his teeth behind his lips. This consequence took the shape of a serious reinforcement schedule. Reinforcement schedules are schedules where rewards are provided in either fixed or intermittent intervals. Typically, schedules have a set time or interval for reinforcement. With Tino, we started with a fixed interval of 3 minutes. That meant every 3 minutes, we were reminded to catch Tino engaging in the keeping-teeth-behind-the-lips behavior. When we caught Tino keeping his teeth behind his lips, he earned a point. Three points earned him a reward menu. Tino could pick a reward from this menu and spend 5 minutes engaged with whatever he had selected. This approach was completely dependent on how motivating the rewards were for Tino. In Appendix L, there is a basic reinforcement/reward checklist to help you and the student find what is motivating for them. Reinforcement inventories are essential. It has been my experience that we may presume to know what a child is motivated by. It is very good practice to include the parents and the child in the rewards selection process.

The inventory led us down an interesting road with Tino. I honestly can't remember how we discovered this (other than a bunch of teaming and problem solving with his parents), but we found out that Tino really loved holding on to and manipulating rubber bike tires—but not just any rubber bike tires, *white* rubber bike tires. There was a stretch of 2 or 3 weeks when Tino was really making progress with his keeping-teeth-behind-the-lips behavior.

We executed these consequences and "rigged the race" as best we could for a few months, and sure enough, Tino's breast biting went down and keeping teeth behind the lips went up. Now that we had completed steps A (tweaking the environment), B (identifying behaviors we wanted to see increase and decrease), and C (delivering consistent and immediate consequences for target behaviors to increase or decrease), we could get down to business about what Tino was trying to communicate with his behavior. The final step of this ABA-based process includes cracking the code behind what bad behavior is trying to communicate. ABA posits that all behaviors serve a purpose or have a function. The good news is that according to ABA, there are only four possible functions or purposes of behavior. This is very reassuring when faced with an overwhelming, complicated, and dangerous behavior. It is kind of nice to know that no matter what, we have to deal with only four options.

The Four Functions of Behavior

According to ABA, every human being engages in any and all behaviors to (1) gain attention, (2) escape an unwanted/undesired activity, (3) gain access to a tangible resource, or (4) because it feels good (or all of the above). There is nothing wrong with wanting to gain attention or get out of something we don't like or gain access to stuff we like or do stuff that feels good.

The problems arise when we go after these things in maladaptive or inappropriate ways. Fortunately, most of us figure out how to achieve these goals without causing too much friction. For instance, if we want someone's attention, we may gently tap their shoulder, raise our hand, or say hello. If we want to get out of an uncomfortable or difficult situation, we may ask for a break. If we want a pair of new shoes, we may buy them. If we want to listen to music really loud, we may use headphones.

The kids with whom we work struggle to figure out how to perform these functions appropriately. Many of them are very aware that they are causing problems; they just don't know how to fix it. Most children who are struggling in one way or another typically operate on a continuum of having either a skill deficit or a performance deficit. In other words, some kids simply don't have any clue how to get their needs met (skill deficit), whereas other kids know how to get their needs met, but they need more practice (performance deficit).

Our job in this situation is to help them identify a better means to the end. When a student is chronically interrupting the class to do something funny or shocking, there's a good chance they are trying to gain attention from the teacher and/or peers. We've got to help that student figure out how to get attention without disrupting the classroom. If a student throws a giant fit when we ask them to finish their assignment, there's a good chance they are trying to escape that assignment. We've got to help that student figure out how to get out of an assignment more appropriately. If a student is stealing from the classroom, they are probably trying to get access to something they want. We have to help the student find a better way to obtain things they want. If a student is humming the same sound over and over again, they are probably getting some sort of stimulation or self-soothing benefit out of it. We have to help them find a time and a place to engage in the humming that won't disturb others or prevent them from learning important concepts in class.

Referring back to Tino, we had to determine the function of his breast-biting behavior. Interestingly, after a few days of observation (and sadly, a few too many bites), we came to the conclusion that the motivation behind the biting was a mix of attention and stimulation. It appeared through our observations that Tino struggled with impulsivity and perhaps some sensory dysregulation. When Tino had acted on the impulse to bite the closest thing to him, it had happened to be Jody's breast. The sensation of biting appeared to have been reinforced by the loud, shrieking reaction to the bite. With Tino, it was almost like he had a little feedback loop and he just wanted that loop to go on and on from bite to scream to bite to scream. I can't tell you why exactly this was the case, but we did test our hypothesis.

We gave Tino a healthy dose of praise (think of a happy scream) and attention for keeping his teeth behind his lips, and at random intervals (when he was caught keeping his teeth behind his lips), he was able to have his white bike tire. Tino would handle the tire and on occasion give it a bite. It was our conclusion that the attention and the biting sensation were the functions of his behavior and once he had those itches scratched, he gave up on the breast biting; he got his fix in a more appropriate way. (We reduced the bike tire by clipping a half inch off every other week, until it was small enough to fit inside his pocket. That way, he wasn't carrying around a tire all day, and when he needed a fix, he could just reach in his pocket.)

The Trick

When working with aggressive children, the trick is discovering the function of their behavior and then teaching them how to reach that goal in an acceptable manner. (It's kind of corny, but the Greek root of *discipline* is related to *disciple*. Our job is not to punish kids who are acting out but to teach them, plain and simple.) This process of identifying a function is referred to as a functional behavioral assessment (FBA). While commonly tossed around in special education and ABA circles, FBAs are not reserved exclusively for those disciplines. I tend to think they can be used for any and all behavior concerns by anyone anytime. Please share these steps with your team.

The Bottom Line

When aggressive behavior becomes a crisis, we typically don't have a lot of time to assess the child's level of happiness, flow state, or otherwise. When breasts are getting bitten or faces are getting scratched, we need to act and we need to act quickly. By following the ABC sequence and identifying plausible functions of the behavior, we can create an intervention plan in a relatively short time. In public schools, our ability to conduct a proper FBA and draft a behavior intervention plan (BIP) that includes positive behavior supports and strives to teach positive replacement behaviors, while monitoring progress, is one of the only legally defensible practices we have when it comes to managing aggressive students. So to help you in these endeavors, you will find in this book an FBA form (Appendix M) and a BIP template (Appendix N). Additionally, Appendix O provides a sleek infographic detailing some of the most common methods of data collection and progress monitoring when addressing aggressive behavior.

READY-TO-USE TOOLS (CHAPTER 5)

I. **The Replacement Behavior Race (Appendix K)**

   <u>What:</u> A worksheet designed to walk you through every single step involved in teaching a positive replacement behavior.

   <u>Why:</u> Far too often, our immediate efforts focus exclusively on trying to decrease the negative or maladaptive behavior. Certainly, those behaviors will require attention; however, the overarching goal of behavior management is to teach a positive replacement behavior to completely eliminate the negative behavior.

How to use it right now: Fill in the blanks for the "Lane 1" and "Lane 2" behaviors. The steps are numbered and go in order. Once you reach the "checkered flag," you have a legally defensible positive replacement behavior plan. Tips to collect data and monitor progress are attached, too!

II. **Reinforcement Checklist (Appendix L)**

What: This inventory catalogs consequences for both good and bad behavior across common categories.

Why: Sometimes you just need a few ideas to get going. Use this inventory with the individual student or their parents to get ideas about things they may be motivated to work for. Also review ideas that serve as consequences for bad behavior.

How to use it right now: Take the inventory and review it with your target student. If they are nonverbal (or perhaps noncompliant), ask folks who know them well to pick from the list.

III. **Functional Behavioral Assessment Form (Appendix M)**

What: This template is designed to provide you with a basic method to conduct an ABC analysis and determine the function of a behavior.

Why: Functional behavioral assessments help you get to the bottom of a behavior problem. The results of the assessment will help guide your decisions about how to help prevent the problem from happening again and how to respond if and when it does.

How to use it right now: Start at the beginning and keep going. The steps are numbered and ordered; all you have to do is answer the questions. Use the results to help guide the content of your behavior intervention plan (Appendix N).

IV. **Sample Behavior Intervention Plan Write-Up (Appendix N)**

What: A basic skeleton outline of how to write a behavior intervention plan and tips on how to organize the content.

Why: Putting everything down on paper or in a document can be time-consuming.

How to use it right now: If you plug all the information from Appendix K into this template, you'll have a plan ready to deliver to your school team tomorrow!

Optimistic Teaming

Just keep swimming. . . .

—Dory, *Finding Nemo* (2003)

One evening, my wife and I were watching the Food Network. I honestly can't remember the name of the show, but the celebrity chef was Jamie Oliver, a young English chef whose claim to fame was making fresh, tasty, stripped-down dishes. In this particular episode, Mr. Oliver was working with some school lunch personnel to take the school lunch budget and buy healthier options for students (e.g., chicken legs versus chicken patties). This seemingly tepid and harmless premise triggered a significant panic attack for me. I got sweaty and nauseated, and my heart started racing. I rose from the couch and abruptly turned off the television.

My bewildered wife looked at me for an explanation. I had no immediate answer, because I was just as surprised as she was by my reaction. It took me a while to settle down and gather my wits. After a few deep breaths and some reflection, I determined that for the previous few weeks, I had been getting stressed out at work. I had been assigned to work with Fenton. Fenton was a 14-year-old male with a penchant for noncompliance and defiance. Yet my stress wasn't due just to the difficulty of working with Fenton. I think most of my stress and anxiety was coming from working with Fenton's school team. The vibe on Fenton's team was not positive. More and more frequently, I was hearing refrains such as, "What's the point? Fenton should not be at school—period!" and "Why should we change everything we're doing for one kid?"

Poor Jamie Oliver was hearing the same resistance from his lunch team: "What's the point? After you leave, we're just gonna serve patties again. . . ." It was too much for me. I may have just been extra sensitive, but Jamie Oliver's struggle really hit close to home. As I watched him, I experienced some sort of weird transference. I ached for just a little bit of optimism. Not only did I ache for this celebrity chef; I ached for me! I needed a little daylight, a little sunshine, you know?

Inevitably, we will encounter school teams presenting some resistance to implementing a new or different behavioral strategy. I try my best to be sympathetic to the teachers on the front lines faced with difficult student behavior. I come from a family of lifelong educators, and I like to believe that I am sensitive to the demands associated with managing a classroom. My approach has always required a delicate balance, though. As much as I want to avoid complicating a teacher's life through behavior management, sometimes there is just no getting around it. My experience has led me to believe that complicated and intense student behavior may require complicated and intense support. Very rarely has a basic strategy worked for extremely difficult students. So when we have to organize a team to address student behavior, it typically involves meeting sometime before school (early) or after school (late) to discuss and troubleshoot. In other words, teacher teams get slammed with the ultimate double whammy: (1) extremely disruptive student and (2) additional time spent in meetings. Thus, it should come as no surprise that school teams can demonstrate some resistance when asked to tackle a behavior intervention plan.

RESISTANCE OR LACK OF TRUST?

I used to chalk up resistance from the school team to personality traits (stubbornness) and limited resources (lack of training). However, the more time I have spent organizing teams to address difficult behavior, the more I have found that most teachers are not resistant to the idea of helping a student. Most of the time, teachers and school teams are resistant to the unknown, being dictated to, or because they do not understand the approach from their standpoint. My observations are not my own. An entire body of research literature exists around confronting resistance and motivation in organizations (and individuals), ranging from the writings of Nobel Prize winner Daniel Kahneman (2002) to Carol Dweck's (2008) *Mindset* and Thaler and Sunstein's (2008) *Nudge*, and everything in between.

As such, it is important to understand that most school teams (and most of us) just want assurances and safeguards prior to attempting something new. Educators are no dummies, and they want some assurances for their investment of time (which may very well be their most valuable commodity). The assurances most school teams desire come in the form of strong follow-through and a proven track record. There is much less resistance from school teams when they know you care enough to follow up and have proven your skills by actually "walking the walk" over simply "talking the talk."

Following up and modeling your proposed strategies in a real-life setting will provide the assurances most teachers require to overcome any resistance. The follow-up and assistance mostly help alleviate their anxieties and stress. With those two barriers kept at bay, most teachers are primed to become invaluable teammates.

WHEN FACING A REVOLT . . .

Truth be told, resistance and dissent related to behavior plans can totally happen. I don't think it happens that often, but I've been on the receiving end of a straight-up mutiny before. While team revolts and mutinies may be rare, it is not unheard of for groups of well-educated professionals to create factions of dissent (Pittenger, 2015; Quinn, 2015; Thornton, 2015). It turns out, when school teams (or any teams, for that matter) decide to dissent and resist contributing to a goal, it is usually due to the following issues: (1) lack of shared vision, (2) psychological contract breaches, and (3) low-quality relationships.

Summoning Your Inner Leader

The lack of shared vision can be addressed by comparing and contrasting the two most common leadership styles found in school settings, known as transformational leadership and transactional leadership. The trick is knowing when to be a transformational leader and when to be a transactional leader. Whether you like it or not, if you are organizing a behavior plan and you need team members to take on responsibility—you're a leader. You're going to need to be assertive and adopt a leadership style. In the school setting, it is common to encounter one of these two possible leadership styles. Table 4 compares and contrasts them.

Our role on the school team will most likely be something like a consultant or team leader/team organizer. There's just no other way to cut it. This can be problematic, because I'm not sure how many of us signed up

Table 4   Transformational Versus Transactional Leadership Styles

Transformational Leadership	*Transactional Leadership*
Charisma: Degree to which the leader behaves in admirable ways that cause team members to identify with the leader	Contingent reward: Providing team members rewards and reinforcement for achieving goals
Inspirational motivation: The degree to which the leader articulates a vision that is appealing and inspiring to team members	Management by exception (active): Closely monitoring team members' behavior, anticipating problems, and taking corrective action
Intellectual stimulation: Degree to which the leader challenges assumptions, takes risks, and solicits team members' ideas	Management by exception (passive): Waiting until the behavior has created problems before taking action
Individualized consideration: Attentiveness to team members' needs	

Adapted from Judge and Piccolo (2004).

to take on leadership roles. Many of us enjoy our behind-the-scenes roles because they are more comfortable. It has been my experience that we can do much more good and be much more effective stepping out from behind the scenes and attempting our best shot at transformational (and when necessary, transactional) leadership.

As a transformational leader, enlist the steps from Table 4 to build a true vision that explains the why (students deserve to be happy), the where (here at school and beyond), and the how (through a plan where we all work together, valuing each other's opinions).

The Psychological Contract Dilemma

It sounds weird (and it is kind of weird), but many of us operate under unwritten rules or invisible social contracts. Some researchers call these psychological contracts (Argyris, 1960; Levinson, Price, Munden, Mandl, & Solley, 1962; Rousseau, 1989, 1995; Schein, 1965; Shore et al., 2004; Taylor & Tekleab, 2004). School teams will resist and dissent when they feel like these invisible contracts have been broken or breached. Essentially, when team members feel like their organization has failed to fulfill its obligations and promises, their invisible contract is broken and they feel like taking a stand. Unfortunately, we don't have much control over this, because the psychological contracts are, well, psychological. Perception is reality for most of us, and if a team member (or an entire team) feels as though our involvement and our plans breach their invisible contract, they may flat out revolt. So the best we can do when this happens is (1) show concern, (2) provide justification or explanation, and (3) take action to deal with the situation. It is tempting to let sleeping dogs lie when we're feeling the heat. Instead of avoiding the problem, honestly attempt to resolve it and form a new unwritten contract.

High-Quality Relationships = High-Quality School Teams

While I am operating on some assumptions stating that high-quality relationships equal high-quality school teams, I think these assumptions are safe. The first assumption is that human beings are social (Maslow, 1968). The second assumption is that social connections are dynamic and change as individuals' feelings and behavior change (Gable & La Guardia, 2007). Third, school teams create "a team" through social processes and a shared understanding. Fourth, there is varying quality to these social connections.

A recent meta-analysis has suggested that these social connections or relationships are impactful in the workplace (Chiaburu & Harrison, 2008). While these analyses are important, I just haven't found anyone who describes the beauty, art, and science behind relationships as well as John Gottman.

Granted, Dr. Gottman is a marriage-and-family guru, but the fact that his work is so frequently referenced across multiple disciplines is a testament to his wisdom. It is also worth noting that he and his institute are constantly reminding folks like me that his work has been researched only in intimate partnerships—not the workplace, not with school teams, and so on. Still, it is too good not to mention. (I'll let you decide the applications with your school team on your own.)

The Sound Relationship House Theory (Gottman & Silver, 2000) basically suggests that if we want to improve a relationship, we should take the following steps (I've adapted the wording a tiny bit to make it more relevant to school-based practitioners):

1. Build a relationship map: Create a road map of each team member's inner world. Try to get to know each other and periodically update this knowledge.

2. Share fondness and admiration: Avoid scanning the team member for mistakes, and instead acknowledge what the team member is doing right and build a culture of appreciation.

3. Turn toward: Fight the temptation to turn away from the needs of your team member, and turn toward their needs.

4. The positive perspective: Define shared interests with each other and attempt to create a friendship, or at least a step above "coworker."

5. Manage conflict: Identify the core issues and the anatomy of repeating negative cycles within the team. Try your best not to repeat these cycles.

6. Help aspirations come true: Understand each other's goals, and work to celebrate and reach them.

7. Create shared meaning: Work to match each other's priorities. If the team shares the same priorities, the sky is the limit!

I know this is marriage-and-family stuff, but honestly, relationships are relationships and I think Dr. Gottman's work is worth considering when faced with a potential mutiny or zero buy-in.

OPTIMISM PREDICTS SUCCESS

Ever since my Jamie Oliver–induced panic attack, I've made a concerted effort to bring as much optimism to teams as possible. For a few years, my optimistic outlook was mostly a survival mechanism. In the world of mental health and behavior management, things can get downright depressing. Oftentimes, if we don't laugh, we will cry. So for a few years, I pressed on, trying to find the silver lining in multiple conflicts and crises. As I am sure you can relate, my stamina for keeping the glass half-full perspective became harder to sustain over time. This became particularly difficult the more frequently I was faced with a challenging student and a grumpy school team.

Fortunately, I received an incredibly potent shot in the arm from the research of V. Mark Durand. Dr. Durand presented his research in a large ballroom with very little fanfare but a tantalizing title: *The Role of Optimism in Improved Outcomes With Positive Behavior Support*. In a giant conference with hundreds of workshops and presentations, this one drew a crowd of practitioners because we knew. We knew deep down that there was so much more to success than a well-drafted behavior plan.

As I sat in the room full of scholars from around the world (this took place at the International Meeting for Autism Research in 2015), Dr. Durand pitched the following question to the group: "If you could guess, what is the single strongest predictor of a successful behavioral intervention?" I couldn't resist, I raised my hand and said something like, "Treatment fidelity." I trusted evidence-based plans and strategies so much that surely their success could be predicted only by how faithfully practitioners implemented them, right? Dr. Durand nodded respectfully and listened to a few more responses. Then he said, *"The single greatest predictor of a successful behavioral intervention is optimism."*

Durand continued by stating that on their own, our precious evidence-based positive behavior support plans produced successful outcomes only about 50% to 66% of the time (Carr et al., 1999). It is worth noting that many of those percentages were collected from controlled settings—not the real-life classroom! So even with our strongest strategies, we are basically flipping a coin to see if they are going to work or not. No school team should be satisfied with those odds.

OPERATIONALIZING OPTIMISM

Durand and his team have investigated the role of optimism working with thousands of teams over many years and have made the following recommendations without hesitation: When attempting to address problem behavior, (1) find out why the student is misbehaving (hopefully, Chapters 1 and 5 in this book have helped out there) and (2) find out if the thoughts and feelings of team members are getting in the way of their being successful student behavior managers.

Since I believe Chapters 1 and 5 in this book do a fine job of explaining why some students punch you in the face, all I really want to cover in this section is ways to help team members who may be struggling. You may cringe a little at the idea of talking about team members' feelings. I get it. However, if we skip this step, we open the door to let a few elephants in the room. These elephants just sort of hang out and watch us make very little (if any) progress toward the improvement of student behavior. So yeah, we gotta talk about the elephants in the room and about each other's feelings. Not because we are pretending to be therapists, but because we need to. Durand's optimistic team strategies help behavioral interventions succeed at a statistically higher rate than using just evidence-based positive behavior intervention (Durand, 2015).

Table 5 provides Durand's (2011) top ten tips for improving optimism on a team.

Appendix P includes a basic worksheet that facilitates the discussion of any perceived elephants in the room. This process may or may not be necessary; however, if you are confronted with some team negativity or unhealthy pessimism, the ability to discuss team optimism levels will be just as important as (or even more so than) enlisting some great plan. In addition to the ability to actually have a discussion about team optimism, it is helpful to know where the optimism/pessimism battles are most commonly waged.

Table 5 Durand's Top Ten Tips to Optimistic Teaming

Tip		Rationale
1	Explore your thoughts and feelings before, during, and after outbursts.	Practice noticing these feelings so you can see later if they help or hurt your teaching skills. Most teachers need help doing this in a way that is productive.
2	If your team member doesn't help, ask why.	Just as your thoughts and feelings interfere with good teaching, so might your team member's self-doubts or doubts about the student. This involves the seemingly obvious but often very difficult issue that confronts most teams—communication.
3	Believe you are a good teacher.	When you add up all you do for your students, the positives far outweigh any occasional lapses you may experience. Focus on the positives.
4	Believe the student can change.	All our experiences tell us any child can improve his or her challenging behavior. It helps to believe this and expect more from your student.
5	Take care of yourself.	You cannot help your student if you are hurting. Give yourself permission to be selfish occasionally.
6	Leverage—don't multitask.	Doing two things at once means you may be doing two things poorly. If you are stretched, try combining activities with your student that achieve multiple goals (e.g., have your student help set up an activity, which gets the activity set up but also provides a learning experience).
7	Teach in the moment.	Keep reminding yourself to focus on what is happening right now with your student (e.g., working independently) rather than other things (e.g., thinking about what will happen at the next transition).
8	Recognize and appreciate the good things in life.	We sometimes have a tendency to focus too much on negative events (e.g., aggressive outburst in the hallway) rather than the positive ones (e.g., participating in group work). Each day, practice reminding yourself the good things that happened that day.
9	Express gratitude toward those people who help you.	One of the most powerful exercises in becoming a happier person is expressing gratitude. Thanking those who help you with your student (including principals, paraprofessionals) will make you feel better and will make the other person feel better as well.
10	Sometimes bad is okay.	Feeling bad sometimes is inevitable for everyone. Accept the fact that there will be down times, and don't fight them. As they say, what doesn't kill you will make you stronger.

From Dr. V. Mark Durand's presentation *The Role of Optimism in Improved Outcomes With Positive Behavior Support*, given at the International Meeting for Autism Research, 2015. Reproduced with permission.

THE PESSIMISM AND OPTIMISM BATTLEFRONTS

Durand and his team have identified seven areas where our optimistic and pessimistic thoughts wage a war with each other—the battlefronts, if you will. The first battlefront where optimistic versus pessimistic thoughts really impact us is the area of self-efficacy, or how we see ourselves as practitioners. The second area or battleground is our concerns about others, or what we think others think about us. The third battleground of pessimism and optimism is the perceptions of the child, or the judging or blaming of parents and/or our classroom management. The fourth battlefront is the area of child efficacy, or the child's perceived ability to control their behavior (e.g., "He did that on purpose!"). The fifth battlefront is the area of pervasiveness, or how frequently the behavior problem occurs. The sixth battlefront is stability, or understanding that the period of aggression was temporary and not ongoing. The seventh battlefront is responsibility, or who/what is to blame for the aggressive outburst.

As in most battlefronts, sometimes the best defense is a good offense. The best weapon we have to help optimism find victory on the battlefield is thought substitution. Appendix Q provides a valuable exercise in thought substitution. Basically, across these areas, we have a tendency to allow pessimistic thoughts to creep in. The trick in thought substitution is to recognize a pessimistic thought and then replace it with a more optimistic one. The practice of substituting pessimistic thoughts with optimistic thoughts has been proven for many years to be a successful approach (Beck & Fernandez, 1998; Hoffmann, 2011).

Appendix Q can become a valuable activity for team members struggling or stuck in a funk in regard to student behavior. It has been my experience that we all need a shot of positivity now and then. Prior to encountering Durand's work, I had never had a strong enough rationale to address unhealthy pessimism directly with team members. Once I understood that pessimism with behavioral strategies actually contributes to their failure, and optimism actually is the strongest predictor of success—I had all the talking points I needed. Those talking points have been included in Appendix Q; do not hesitate to use them when you encounter obstructionist negativity in a team.

READY-TO-USE TOOLS (CHAPTER 6)

I. Behavior Data Infographic (Appendix O)

<u>What:</u> An infographic explaining common methods to progress monitor behavior data.

<u>Why:</u> Establishing a plan for an aggressive student takes work and, more often than not, requires a little more from the teachers working

with the aggressive student. Any team member will balk at a strategy where there is no follow-up or support—and could you blame them? By establishing 2-week-chunk follow-ups, you build a relationship of trust and accountability with team members.

How to use it right now: Review and share with team members and come up with a way (with crayons or a spreadsheet) to demonstrate a baseline (dates and behaviors *prior* to the new behavior plan), and then monitor up to two consecutive weeks of the plan. Measure behaviors you want to see increase and behaviors you want to see decrease.

II. **"Hello There, Elephant" Worksheet (Appendix P)**

What: A basic communication facilitation worksheet that formalizes the process of team-based problem solving as it relates to pessimistic attitudes.

Why: Sometimes the things we don't talk about are the exact things we need to fix for real change to happen. By formalizing this process as a normal step in the creation of the behavior plan, teams can begin talking about the roles their individual attitudes play in the successful outcome of a behavioral intervention.

How to use it right now: This worksheet is probably best used preventively. Introduce this worksheet early on in the behavior intervention planning process. That way, it becomes part of a formal process as opposed to a reactionary process that may put you and your team members on the defensive. This doesn't mean you can't bring it in after a plan has started, when some pessimistic team members start spreading the dread. It is helpful to have this tool at the ready and address the harm of pessimism on the successful outcome of a strategy.

III. **Thought Replacement Exercises (Appendix Q)**

What: Basic exercises in challenging our cognition. These exercises are prompts. Simply practice replacing the pessimistic thought/view with an optimistic one.

Why: Pessimistic thoughts can creep in at any time. Keeping those thoughts at bay or substituting them with optimistic thoughts may be the difference in the successful outcome of your behavior plan.

How to use it right now: Review the prompts and give them a whirl! This is not just a cutesy exercise; these activities will help you and your team actually become more optimistic. The more optimistic you and your team are, the more likely your behavioral intervention will be successful. Successful behavioral interventions mean less aggression and—you guessed it—happier kids.

Bringing It All Together

The Step-by-Step "Happy Kids Don't Punch You in the Face" Process

Ain't nothin' to it but to do it!

—Ronnie Coleman (2000)

For those of you who have skipped ahead to this chapter, I get it. I take no offense; in fact, there is some research suggesting that skipping to the end of a book may actually enhance your experience (Christenfeld & Leavitt, 2011). Of course, that research investigated only three types of books (ironic-twist, mystery, and literary). I don't know the impact of books focusing on research, theory, and practice for addressing student aggression in schools. (I bet you're okay though.)

However, if we assume that skipping ahead does indeed enhance your experience, I will choose to believe that your enhanced experience came from implementing these strategies, loving them, and then going back and reading about where they came from! (Yes, that makes me feel better.)

Well, regardless of how or why you have arrived at this chapter, we must first acknowledge the two most important factors in working with students exhibiting aggression and/or dangerous behavior: safety and the law.

STEP 1: SAFETY AND THE LAW

Getting injured by aggressive students is a real risk for those who work in public schools (Tiesman, Konda, Hendricks, Mercer, & Amandus, 2014). Tiesman et al. found from a statewide study that 309 of 2,514 educators were assaulted a combined 597 times. Special education teachers, urban educators, and educators in their first 3 years of employment were at an increased risk. The authors found that while most assaults did not lead to medical care or time away from work, those assaulted were significantly more likely to find work stressful, have low job satisfaction, and consider leaving the education field.

It will be critical for you and your school team to understand and review your school district's policy and procedures for when employees are assaulted by a student. There has been some general guidance from the U.S. Department of Education to inform policy and procedure, but let me get right down to it: You need to ensure that faculty and staff are appropriately trained in positive behavior supports and effective crisis response to aggressive student behavior. There is no question that physical restraint and seclusion have been deemed the ultimate and last resort when responding to student aggression.

We all agree that these protections are necessary, even more so when students identified with disabilities are involved. Our students with disabilities warrant and deserve the highest-quality protections and services we can provide. So to help you out, I've organized a pretty comprehensive overview of the federal guidelines for working with children of all abilities in the school setting.

Your Legal Briefing

In the most recent and comprehensive review of public school responses to difficult student behavior, U.S. Secretary of Education Arne Duncan provided 15 guiding principles that "stress every effort to prevent the need for the use of restraint and seclusion and that any behavior intervention must be consistent with the child's rights to be treated with dignity and to be free from abuse" (U.S. Department of Education, 2012).

Simply put, the U.S. Department of Education (2012) has declared:

> *Physical restraint or seclusion should not be used except in situations where the child's behavior poses imminent danger of serious physical harm to self or others and other interventions are ineffective and should be discounted as soon as imminent danger of serious physical harm to self or others has dissipated.* (p. 2)

So it is up to your respective state education authority (state board of education) and your local educational authority (district school board or charter) to create a policy and procedure for when student behavior "poses imminent danger of serious physical harm." No matter what, your district must have (a) a system for documenting serious student aggression, (b) guidelines for the use of an emergency procedure such as physical restraint, and (c) procedures that notify parents "as soon as possible" (U.S. Department of Education, 2012). Now, wouldn't it be great if you had a comprehensive, engaging training complete with mnemonic devices to teach and train faculty and staff what to do when a student "poses imminent danger of serious physical harm"?

STEP 2: STAY SAFE WITH A COMPREHENSIVE, ENGAGING TRAINING COMPLETE WITH MNEMONIC DEVICES TO TEACH AND TRAIN FACULTY AND STAFF WHAT TO DO WHEN A STUDENT "POSES IMMINENT DANGER OF SERIOUS PHYSICAL HARM"

For the past few years, I have been slowly transitioning from my role as first responder to behavioral crises to a more consultative role. In my current capacity as an administrator and trainer, there has been an expectation that my methods be replicated by more and more professionals. Honestly, this entire book is designed to be the source material for training colleagues, parents, and any other stakeholder. I have crafted a comprehensive professional development program that uses the train-the-trainer model (Fremouw, 1975; Gresham, 1989; Hester, Kaiser, Alpert, & Whiteman, 1996) so school districts can become certified in the "Happy Kids" approach. None of us can help a student by ourselves; it really does take a village. (You're just going to have to train the entire village.)

Supplementary to the content preceding this chapter, I have created comprehensive training modules for school-based practitioners tasked with working with aggressive student behavior. I wanted the modules to be as straightforward and reproducible as possible. I even came up with a cute little acronym (ASPEN, to honor the lovely trees that cover the mountains near my home). For the past decade, I have been training numerous school districts and charter schools on the ASPEN procedures listed below:

> **A**—*Assess the situation and ask for assistance.* School personnel should be trained to evaluate the seriousness of the situation in a split second. The level of seriousness should be determined by any

imposing threat of harm and whether or not the threat is real (manifesting in the environment), immediate (happening right now in front of you), and capable of causing harm (elementary-age students are rarely capable of causing serious harm unless weapons are involved or they are engaging in elopement, running toward a parking lot or traffic). School personnel should also be trained to ask for assistance immediately. It is never a good idea to be alone when a student is becoming aggressive.

S—*Select a course of action.* School personnel should be trained to attempt either a nonverbal or verbal de-escalation strategy, prior to calling the police or engaging in any sort of physical restraint. The nonverbal strategy includes steps to remain calm and not confront the aggressive student. School personnel should be trained that nonverbal communication is typically delivered through body language (e.g., relaxed, nonthreatening posture), which can subtly communicate compassion and understanding—not to mention a perceived sense of control. Interestingly, the perceived sense of control can be crucial when a student acts *out* of control. Buried deep behind the student's aggression will be some measure of relief that at least *someone* is in control. Verbal de-escalation is simply a firm, clear command to calm down and an opportunity to remind the student that you are there to help.

P—*Is physical assistance even necessary?* School personnel should be trained that prior to confronting a student emergency with some form of physical restraint or assistance, they must evaluate the reasoning behind such a step. The threat of harm must be real, immediate, and capable of causing real harm, prior to executing physical assistance. Very rarely is physical assistance even warranted. However, personnel should be trained in a physical restraint procedure to follow if the threat is real, immediate, and capable of causing real harm. School personnel must be trained that physical restraint procedures are the last resort. Additionally, school personnel should be trained to avoid attempting physical restraint with any student of their same height or weight. School personnel should be instructed to contact the police if the student is their height or taller.

E—*Explain and engage.* School personnel should be trained to say, "I am going to touch you," prior to engaging in any physical restraint. This step provides notice and warning prior to any physical contact. The human rights of students require some attempt to give the student notice that physical contact is imminent (as long as the threat continues to be real, immediate, and capable of causing harm).

N—*Neutrally disengage.* This step should train school personnel to safely disengage from the student by avoiding any conversation with or emotional response to the student throughout the emergency situation. Additionally, this step should train school personnel how to release the student from physical restraint (if and when physical restraint is enlisted).

School districts interested in certifying their faculty and staff in the ASPEN Training Modules are welcome to visit www.totempd.com to schedule a training. ASPEN Training Modules are designed to be delivered directly to faculty and staff from ASPEN certified trainers, or we can certify trainers from your own school in a Train-the-Trainer (TTT) model. The TTT model is ideal for building sustainability of these practices in your school setting. Each of the ASPEN Training Modules includes access to a Train-the-Trainer Handbook, Presentation Materials, and Booster Training Materials to offer multiple times throughout the school year.

STEP 3: PREPARE TO BE A RESOURCE FOR SCHOOL TEAMS, PARENTS, AND COLLEAGUES

Review the contents of this book and be prepared to be a resource for your school team regarding aggressive student behavior. What does a good-quality resource need to have prepared?

1. Ready-to-use strategies

2. Explanations for dumbfounded parents and colleagues about why the aggression took place and how to stop it from happening again (Appendix A)

3. An inventory of stakeholders' top five behavioral concerns for the student (While you may have your own hunches about what behaviors should be addressed first, if you fail to take inventory with those folks on the front lines with the students, it can have a negative impact on the success of your plan.)

STEP 4: BUILD RAPPORT AND SPEND SOME QUALITY TIME WITH THE TARGET STUDENT

The only way we can build rapport with the students with whom we work is to spend some quality time getting to know them. We may or may not have a choice in how much time we spend with the target student (particularly if the student is acting out—we may be assigned to them at some point). Our ability to establish some rapport and genuine respect for each other is crucial. Back in Chapter 2, we discussed how necessary compassion is for taking a behavior plan and creating something lasting for the student. Believe it or not, a research-validated compassionate method of building rapport with difficult students has been around for over a decade. This method has been implemented through a process known as motivational interviewing (Miller & Rollnick, 2004).

The gist behind motivational interviewing (MI) is that it identifies explicit steps involved in building an authentic relationship with difficult kids. The goal of MI is to explore how the target students actually feel about the status quo and about the possibility of change by exploring their values, interests, and concerns. It is incredible how unique MI is when we consider what else is commonly used in school settings: confrontation, education, and authority. MI is supposed to be focused on the student's autonomy, collaboration, and the solicitation of the student's own ideas regarding change. This can be a difficult mindset to adopt if the concern is more about confronting the student or establishing authority.

What are these explicit steps behind MI, then? Well, there are two steps in MI. The first step is the awareness of the stage model of intentional behavior change. According to this model, kids' desire to change can vary across five stages: (1) precontemplation (not yet considering change), (2) contemplation (considering change), (3) preparation (planning and committing change), (4) action (making the behavior change), and (5) maintenance (maintaining and sustaining long-term change). MI requires that practitioners understand what stage the child is in and include that understanding in the drafting of the behavior plan. There is no utility in drafting a behavior plan where Stage 4 (action) is the goal when the student may be in Stage 2 (contemplation), and so on. Taking these small steps to identify what stage the student is working through increases the overall relevance of the behavior plan for the student, which typically results in more compliance to the plan. How can you tell which stage the student is in? By visiting with the student, taking time to observe the student and gather as much information as you can about them. Then evaluate your behavior data and come to a conclusion or best guess. It is a good idea to write the stages down, perhaps on a timeline, and invite team members to hypothesize about where the student falls in regard to the stages. This process can help the team approach the pace and rate of change more realistically.

The second step in MI is best illustrated by a mnemonic tool I use to help me remember each underlying principle of MI. The tool I use is called "SEE RED." (I use this because when interviewing children, it often feels as though all they are seeing is red, like they are on the war path.) Let me break down this tool:

S—*Self-efficacy.* Every interview should be focused on the child's own belief in the possibility of change. The student, not the educator, is responsible for choosing and carrying out change. However, the educator's own belief in the student's ability to change becomes a self-fulfilling prophecy. This first step really comes down to our belief that change is possible (and letting the child know that as well).

E & E—*Express Empathy.* Our interviews should be daily practice of skillful, reflective listening during the child's contemplation stage. We should not get frustrated with students when they express ambivalence—this is a normal response for students. Essentially, it is our job to "be in the moment" with students and try to put ourselves in their shoes.

R—*Roll with resistance.* Interviews with kids are not always the smoothest experience. We have to acknowledge that change is not going to come easy. In fact, we should just plan on some resistance. Resistance should not be directly opposed during the child's contemplation stage. Our job is to invite new perspectives, but not impose them. The student should remain the primary source for answers and solutions. Interestingly, rolling with resistance also prevents our own tendency to burn out or "work harder than our client." Breathe the resistance in, patiently wait for opportunities, then guide the student through choice—not relying on your authority.

E—*Engage.* Our interviewing styles should be planned and strategic, but it is important to let our guard down a bit and attempt to relate to the student on a human level. While we must acknowledge the behavioral tenets of ABA by providing clear and consistent boundaries, there should always be a moment in the interview where we are genuinely interested in getting to know more about the student.

D—*Develop discrepancy.* The catalyst for change (for most of us) is motivated by a perceived discrepancy between our present behavior and our important goals or values. In other words, we don't get off the train until we understand which stop will get us closer to our goal. The student, rather than the educator, should present arguments for change during the contemplation stage. The difficult part is that many of us working with kids think we know which train stop the student should exit—and maybe we're right; the problem is that the student has to figure that out. Our job is to evaluate all the other stops on the line and help students come to their own conclusions.

STEP 5: FBAS AND BIPS, OH MY!

While functional behavioral assessments (FBAs) and behavior intervention plans (BIPs) are certainly familiar to educators working in special education, they are not reserved just for special education students. FBAs and BIPs can be applied to anything—literally anything—involving behavior. So regardless of whether or not the student exhibiting aggression is eligible for special education, use these strategies and get as much practice and input as you can with them. (Appendices M and N will be very helpful here.)

In addition to your FBA, you must draft a BIP. Do not forget to include information from stakeholders' top five concerns in this plan. The success of BIPs depends in large part on how well the stakeholders feel their concerns are being addressed. In the biz, we call this *social validity* or *consumer satisfaction*. By obtaining their top five concerns, you will be able to prioritize and build in strategies that will resonate with stakeholders and encourage their buy-in and support.

I cannot stress this enough: So many assessments and plans end up being full of jargon and overly technical. This phenomenon is more likely to occur with the highly certified (e.g., Board Certified Behavior Analysts) and über-educated professionals (PhDs) you may come in contact with. For whatever reason, those of us who get trained in the technical realms of behavior management can easily fall in the trap of (a) becoming know-it-alls and (b) writing and speaking in jargon all day. Trust me: Parents and teachers just want help and they want plain, clear instructions on how the help is coming. Please remember this. (Note: You may be highly certified and über-educated in your field, which is fantastic; just don't forget to express your findings and opinions with some good old-fashioned bedside manner.)

We live and work in a relatively new sociopolitical environment wherein parents and teachers know their stuff and have the World Wide Web at their fingertips. So I'm not talking about "dumbing down" the technical aspects of our work; I'm talking about communicating information in a meaningful way.

STEP 6: ESTABLISH THE
FEEDBACK LOOP AND CRISIS TREE

To set the stage for an optimistic and effective team, identify the means and methods by which you will be supporting the implementation of the behavior plan and how frequently you will follow up. Inform the team what data you will be collecting (based on your functional assessment and positive replacement behaviors). Team members may be asked to collect some data with you. Be clear and concise about how and what they should record.

Additionally, take inventory of each other's most common methods of communication and create the ever-important "crisis tree." This is a basic form organized like a phone tree. Provide this chart to the team and fill it out together. The crisis tree informs the team who, when, and why to call in case of an emergency. Remind the team that this is only for an emergency. If behaviors are escalating but there is no immediate emergency, stick to the steps outlined in the BIP.

Share the feedback loop and crisis tree with the student's parents as well as the school principal. Many of the efforts you will be making and working toward will rely on how well you communicate goings-on to parents and the school administrator. The same can be said for the rest of the school team. The cliché "Communication is key" is extremely valid in this step.

STEP 7: MONITOR PROGRESS AND TROUBLESHOOT

If you have successfully completed Step 1 through Step 6 to the best of your ability, your role now is to set up a consistent follow-up schedule wherein you monitor progress and make yourself available for troubleshooting the behavior plan. This step primarily addresses how well you and your team understand the data you are collecting and what you consider to be meaningful progress.

If you've used behaviors from the stakeholders' top five concerns, there is a good chance you are monitoring meaningful data points. From there, progress is anything better than the baseline data (the time before you started the intervention). Honestly, there are so many cool ways to collect and measure data, I could not possibly provide all of them here, and while you can create some amazing Excel spreadsheet or Google Doc, crayons and markers are okay, too. The primary goal is to collect data points across 2-week chunks and display them visually for the stakeholders. (Appendix O provides a very basic example of the visual data presentation I have used frequently.)

I don't feel too confident providing you with an exhaustive troubleshooting list because, frankly, there are too many unique scenarios and kids out there for me to even consider. The primary objective is that you make yourself available to the team to troubleshoot your plan. In an effort to help, below is a list of some common areas that may warrant consideration regarding a student's progress (or lack thereof):

1. What was the student's attendance like for the data-collection period?

   - Erratic attendance will most likely contribute to regression or low-quality improvements.

2. Were there any school breaks within the data-collection period? If so, how many? How long?

   - Monitor the days before and after a break to determine if they correlate with poor behavior.
   - Avoid starting a new plan right before a long break. Good plans require plenty of consistency. Look at the calendar and try to sync the best stretches of time for the best result.
   - If you can't get around it, push through the breaks and increase your communication with the parents about the consistency of the plan.

3. Was any member of the student's team absent? If so, for how long throughout the data-collection period?

   - Determine who was absent and what type of information they will need upon their return.
   - Determine who their replacement is, and work to get their replacement up to speed on the plan.
   - As you collect data, note any differences in behavior with different team members.

4. Was there a substitute teacher for any of the data-collection period? Was the substitute notified of the behavior plan?

   - It is crucial that substitute teachers be debriefed on the nuances of the behavior plan. Take time to visit with substitutes to ensure they follow the major aspects of the plan as best they can.

5. Any significant changes at home (e.g., moving, illness, loss, divorce)?

   - Keep tabs with the parents and home life as best you can. School personnel are not always privy (nor is it expected that they *should* always be privy) to the goings-on at home. If you are aware of certain situations that may have caused increased levels of stress or anxiety, it is worth noting to see if there were any correlations between the stressful event and the behavior.

6. Have the student's diet, exercise, and sleep been considered? Anything unusual across these areas?

   - These areas are often overlooked when difficult behavior is present. In fact, some really intense and weird behavior can simply be the result of a poor diet (e.g., chronic gut/gas pain and indigestion, dehydration, constipation), and little to no exercise can result in challenging behaviors and poor sleep cycles. Inadequate sleep can impact anything from attention and memory to mood.

7. Is the student on any medication? If so, have there been any changes in the dose or lapses?

   • Understanding the pharmacology of certain medications is important, particularly in younger children, as their development is in pretty constant flux. Keep in touch with the student's doctor who prescribed the medication, and when possible, check for any correlations between behaviors monitored at school and changes in the medication regimen.

While in this troubleshooting state of mind, you may encounter some team dissent or pessimism regarding the plan. Appendix P is custom-built to help you address team members who appear to be dissenting or simply not putting their best foot forward in the plan. While it may feel as though you have team members attempting to sabotage or revolt, what is most likely happening is either (1) they do not understand the shared vision of the plan, (2) they feel as though some sort of psychological contract has been broken with the plan, or (3) they have a low-quality relationship with you or someone else on the team. (On some occasions, your team members may be feeling all of the above.) Chapter 6 was written to help you navigate this obstacle if and when it arises. That chapter is essentially your troubleshooting guide if and when you encounter a grumpy team.

STEP 8: KNOW WHEN TO PIVOT

Angela Duckworth, the author of *Grit: The Power of Passion and Perseverance* (2016), has contributed a wealth of information regarding what it takes to trudge through everything life throws at us. Duckworth's research on resilience and "stick-to-it-ness" suggests that our goals be organized in a hierarchy. Figure 4 illustrates the concept of a goal hierarchy for our reference.

Figure 4 illustrates that top-level goals are usually singular and immovable. In other words, our top-level goals for behavior plans should be specific, concrete, and attainable. There should also be a general consensus in the school team for the top-level goal. Then our behavior plans must have mid-level goals that are still precious but somewhat less precious than our top goal. The reasoning is that there may come a time

Figure 4 Duckworth's Goal Hierarchy

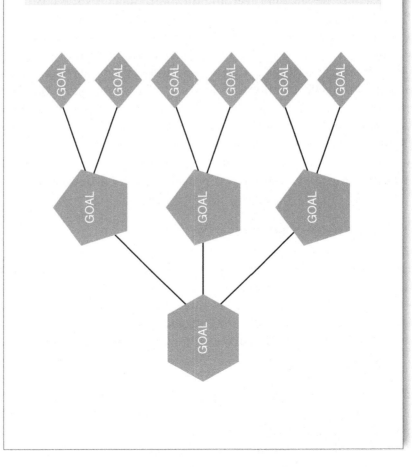

GRIT HIERARCHY

High-Level

Following Duckworth, grit is all about our ability to keep our eyes on a high-level goal. This high-level goal really is nonnegotiable.

Mid-Level

Knowing there are multiple paths to our high-level goal is crucial. Our ability to be flexible at this stage will actually make our high-level goal more attainable.

Low-Level

These low-level goals typically do not last for the duration of our work. Avoid making these goals too precious, because there's a good chance they will need to be changed or disregarded at some point.

Based on research and work by Angela Duckworth (2016).

when a mid-level goal is not reached or is even rejected. Understanding there are multiple ways to our top goal is key to grit and perseverance. (Grit and perseverance are key to successful outcomes.) This understanding is also key to communicating with your team. This is sort of a "you-can't-make-an-omelette-without-breaking-a-few-eggs" perspective. In other words, we can fail and that's okay—if the failure occurs in the low- to mid-level goals.

Now, the low-level goals are the least precious goals of the hierarchy. That doesn't mean they're not important; it's just that as you start out, day to day, don't get discouraged if and when a low-level goal is not reached. When we fail to reach a low- or even mid-level goal, Duckworth (2016) suggests that is when we should pivot:

> When you see your goals organized in a hierarchy, you realize that grit is not at all about stubbornly pursuing—at all costs and ad infinitum—every single low-level goal on your list. In fact, you can expect to abandon a few of the things you're working very hard on at this moment. Not all of them will work out. Sure, you should try hard—even a little longer than you might think necessary. But don't beat your head against the wall attempting to follow through on something that is, merely, a means to a more important end. (p. 68)

In other words, knowing when to pivot from a goal is key to the success of your behavior plan. Take some time to review this concept with your team and open a discussion about what are the low-, mid-, and top-level goals of the behavior plan. Explain to the team and stakeholders that it is okay to abandon low- and even mid-level goals as long as you keep your eyes on the prize.

STEP 9: CELEBRATE SUCCESS AND EXPRESS GRATITUDE

While you can certainly encourage your team members to do the same, I recommend that you or someone on the team enlist V. Mark Durand's "three good things" strategy. This strategy is pretty simple. At the end of each day of the first week of the behavior plan, document three things that went well for the student, you, or even the team. You only have to do this for a week. (I recommend doing it the first week and then maybe during a low-morale week in the future.)

Document even the smallest successes, the causes of those successes, and if you observe any patterns. If you have time, even attempt to briefly describe your reactions to this task and how it made you feel. Share what you discovered with the team through a basic e-mail, group text, or note.

As you document the things going well, be sure to express your gratitude to the team and stakeholders (and even the student!) for helping out. Gratitude is a wonderful phenomenon; those that practice gratitude tend to be happier people. When you model this "attitude of gratitude," there will be plenty of folks watching and learning from your actions, and none more so than the child with whom you are working.

STEP 10: REFINE AND REPEAT

Take time to review the plan and the goals of the team. Ensure that the student is aware of both the plan and the goals. In fact, the student (regardless of age) should be brought up to speed just as frequently as (if not more so than) the rest of the team. There will inevitably be glitches in the plan and things that require reconfiguration. Just keep track of those refinements and see which refinements (or dare we say, *pivots*) work, and document their impact toward the overall goal of the team and the progress of the student.

Once we have established what we are refining, we simply start this process all over again from Step 1 through Step 10. No good behavior plan looks the same at the end as it did at the beginning. In other words, modifications are a good sign and are to be expected. But while plan modifications and refinements are a good sign, we must remember that they should not come willy-nilly. We must use our data and team feedback loop to make changes to the plan. Protect the consistency of the plan at all costs, and when you and the team decide to pivot or change components of the plan, be clear about why.

SO WHAT DOES THIS LOOK LIKE?

Table 6 is our checklist of everything we need to have in place to help children increase their joy and decrease their aggression.

It may be helpful to use these "steps to success" as a journal complete with artifacts and a way to organize your priorities. For instance, for every step, keep an artifact that confirms, "Yes, that step has been accomplished." Steps 1 and 2 should include a local education agency (LEA)–approved emergency procedure form that looks something like Appendix R. Appendix R is to be used as a template only. Be sure to review your own LEA policy and procedures about the documentation of an emergency procedure.

Table 6   "Happy Kids Don't Punch You in the Face" Steps to Success

Yes/No	Steps
Y/N	1. Does the team have an emergency procedure to keep everyone safe?
Y/N	2. Is the emergency procedure compliant with federal, state, and local guidelines?
Y/N	3. Has the team been trained in "Happy Kids" research, theory, and practice?
Y/N	4. Has the team been trained in ASPEN de-escalation steps?
Y/N	5. Has the team lead been identified and prepared to be a resource for any/all questions and supports regarding the plan to help the student?
Y/N	6. Has the team lead and/or any other team member spent time building rapport with the target student? Have they used the principles of motivational interviewing (i.e., genuine expression of empathy, development of discrepancy between the student's current behavior and the replacement behavior plan, rolling with the student's resistance, and support of the student's self-efficacy)?
Y/N	7. Has the team lead conducted an FBA and drafted a BIP complete with a positive replacement behavior?
Y/N	8. Has the team created a feedback loop and crisis tree to sustain ongoing communication?
Y/N	9. Has the team identified data points to monitor progress? Is there a process to troubleshoot if there's a lack of progress?
Y/N	10. Does the team understand the concept of "pivoting" from low- and mid-level goals of the behavior plan?
Y/N	11. Is the team celebrating success and expressing gratitude to one another?
Y/N	12. Has the team cycled through the previous steps in order to refine each one?
Y/N	13. Success? Why? Why not?

Step 3 should include a roll with dates, names, and signatures where topics from this book have been discussed with team members. Step 4 should also include a roll with dates, names, and signatures of attendees from an ASPEN-certified training (or at least from some other, less engaging, less fun, more aggressive behavior training). All my bad jokes aside, whatever your LEA chooses to train faculty and staff, choose *something*. LEAs take on a serious amount of risk if they do not explicitly train personnel in managing aggressive and dangerous student behavior. In some states, it may even be the law that LEAs adopt a training procedure to prevent and respond to aggressive student behavior.

Step 5 should include the name and contact information of a team lead or point person. There should probably also be a "next-in-line" name and contact information if the team lead is unavailable. Step 6 should have logs and notes about who has built some rapport with the target student and how. It would be remarkable to provide some hypotheses in the logs and notes about what "change stage" they believe the child is in and what underlying principles of MI they have attempted.

Step 7 is essential. Very clear dated and signed copies of the FBA and drafted BIP should be made available to all team members and kept secure and confidential. Step 8 could be something as simple as a log with dates and times the team has received feedback about the progress of the behavior plan. Additionally, Step 8 should include the names and contact information of team members who can be contacted in case of an emergency or crisis. Step 9 is essential to making any/all decisions pertaining to the behavior plan. Artifacts for this step should be visual, graphic data illustrating the performance of the target student behaviors we want to see increase and decrease.

Step 10 could be something as simple as a goal inventory where the team has decided to pivot or try something a little different while not deviating from a general course of improved behavior. Step 11 could also be a simple log with dates and times when successes were celebrated and reminders to express gratitude to team members.

Step 12 is essentially this checklist. Use the Y/N checklist above to confirm what steps have been completed and what steps may require some refinement. Allow Step 13 to be a bimonthly event. The behavior plan should be evaluated in 2-week chunks (10 school days). Evaluate success or lack thereof regularly and revisit the previous 12 steps to keep your focus on what needs to take place.

Conclusion

Where Are They Now?
Student Snapshots!

TREVOR

I first met Trevor when he was in the first grade. There were some reports about his behavior in the early fall, but I didn't get involved until around October. I had been working in the field long enough to respect that 7-year-olds could be a force to be reckoned with.

Trevor was interesting because he was incredibly intelligent, with a wry sense of humor—and he was 7 years old. His vocabulary was grade levels above that of any first grader I had ever met—and he enjoyed using it. We came to find out that his vocabulary gave the adults in his life a false sense of his emotional maturity levels. Most of us felt that if he could speak with adults, he should be acting like an adult. One of the many issues we discovered was that, emotionally, he was very young, maybe even delayed. That discrepancy took those of us on his team a lot of time to understand.

Trevor's initial repertoire of behavioral outbursts typically included destroying property and physically attacking peers. At the drop of a hat, Trevor could lose his temper and lash out at whatever and whoever was nearby. His zero-to-sixty rage was my indicator that he was entrenched in a coercive cycle. It was as if he were going for broke on every roll of the dice. Helping the team stay consistent and firm in the face of a Trevor meltdown was difficult, but the team did a great job.

As the weeks went by, Trevor's principal and teacher requested (and were provided with) a behavioral aide (a paraprofessional with a background in behavior management). The aide's name was Stefanie. I was happy for any help I could get, and Stefanie was an incredible paraprofessional. (I recently found out from a source—i.e., Facebook— that Stefanie became a successful school psychologist in her own right years later.)

Stefanie and I teamed up with Mrs. Tanney (Trevor's classroom teacher), Mrs. Ocher (Trevor's special education teacher), Mrs. Graywall (Trevor's school counselor), Trevor's parents, Trevor's private therapist, the lunch staff, the recess aides, the media center staff, and the bus staff to provide a positive support plan. (With the exception of Mrs. Tanney, this team stayed relatively similar for the next 3 years.)

Our functional assessments over the years pretty much concluded that Trevor's aggression had three functions: first, to escape work (it turned out the work was too simple for him, and he got bored); second, to gain attention (primarily from adults); and third, to seek stimulation (yes, we found enough evidence to support the idea that there was some sort of stimulating component to his outbursts; it was as if he enjoyed the havoc).

As I mentioned earlier, we didn't see much progress until we started seeing a happier Trevor. I am convinced that Trevor's happiness improved over the years due to the time we spent with him—not just face time but quality rapport-building time. He didn't require a ton of supervision, but when we were available, it was important to have meaningful exchanges with him. Our behavior plans were strong and steady, but holy cow, for the first year, the graphs looked like a heartbeat monitor—peaks and valleys over and over. The lasting improvements did not occur until multiple folks on the team had established some level of rapport with Trevor.

Our plan resulted in placing Trevor in a gifted and talented program within the school (which was unprecedented at the time, because only third graders and up were permitted to participate in the program). In that setting, he was challenged and motivated to pursue activity-based projects. If and when the curriculum became more performance-graded (as opposed to participation-graded), he would engage in more outbursts. We modified those components and mitigated his outbursts significantly over time.

We began fading Stefanie from his side from the beginning. We made it clear to Mrs. Tanney (and his subsequent teachers) that we were nearby and monitoring his behavior, but we did not want to foster any sort of dependence on the aide. This approach paid off, as the last half of his second-grade year and the totality of his third-grade year, Trevor's behavior required only check-ins, not constant supervision.

My favorite part of the plan was the time Trevor and I spent identifying the behaviors we wanted to see decrease (e.g., aggression and non compliance) and the behaviors we wanted to see increase (e.g., keeping hands to self and following directions). We came up with a name for the aggressive behaviors to use as code and to make it easier to communicate to his teachers and team. Trevor was so self-aware that he acknowledged that when he acted aggressively, he felt grandiose and tough; so we labeled anything he did aggressively or oppositionally as "macho nacho" behavior. It didn't make much sense (except for the *macho* part), but for whatever reason, this really stuck with him; he got it. Inversely, we labeled the behaviors we wanted to see increase as "cool cucumber" behaviors. It was fun working with Trevor on labeling his behaviors in these conceptual frameworks. I think that due to his vocabulary and reasoning level, he appreciated and understood what we were attempting to do: bring down the machismo and bring up the ability to relax.

The result? Trevor became a happier kid in school, and soon his ability to cope with his emotional outbursts began to catch up with his ability to reason; the world was his oyster. Like clockwork, Trevor's behaviors fluctuated as his relationships fluctuated. When Trevor felt accepted by his team, he improved. When there were lapses in the quality of rapport with school teams, he regressed. Motivational interviewing and building rapport saved all of us. I learned many things from Trevor: first and foremost, to be real, care, and roll with the resistance; it pays off eventually.

Trevor's behavior data are provided below.

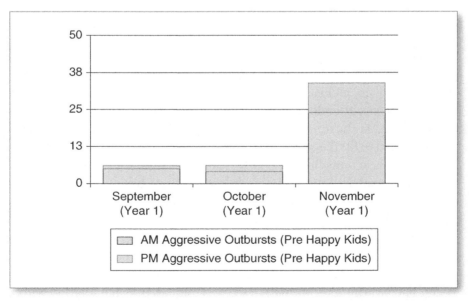

(Continued)

(Continued)

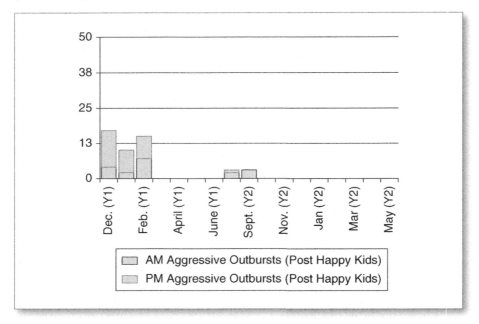

Prior to the "Happy Kids" approach, Trevor was averaging 15 aggressive outbursts a month. After our time together, Trevor averaged two aggressive outbursts through the rest of our first year, with a significant drop-off in our second year.

LUIS

Luis was another smart little fella. Luis fortunately attended a school that incorporated an inclusion model for students with disabilities. In other words, Luis was attending class with everybody else his age, and that was a good thing. At the time, Luis possessed a significant speech and language delay (related to his diagnosis with an autism spectrum disorder), but it was evident in his actions how intensely he enjoyed figuring out the details of his environment. He knew exactly where everything was supposed to be and exactly what time the activities of the day were supposed to take place. Luis's aggression was a problem because it was having a significant impact on his social development. In preschool (and arguably throughout life), peers are not very tolerant to mega-tantrums. It was especially problematic for Luis because we noticed that he was becoming more and more isolated from his peers. The last thing we wanted to see was increased social isolation with a student already predisposed to struggle with social interaction.

The majority of our functional assessments led to a single function: attention. Luis was experiencing delayed language skills and became super frustrated when he couldn't communicate his wants and needs. Many times, Luis would lose control and seemingly decide that aggression was easier than attempting to organize his language.

For the most part, our behavior plans were firm and stable to the best of our ability. The consistency appeared to have a particularly profound impact on Luis's aggressive behavior. It was as if Luis craved the structure despite the fact that the structure included some negative consequences (like a seat away or loss of a privilege).

In preschool-age children, I have seen the most marked improvement in behavior over time—more so than in any other age group or grade level. Clearly there is something to providing early intervention services for preschoolers. Luis made dramatic improvements in conjunction with his speech and language therapy. As Luis's language improved and our plans remained firm and consistent, Luis rarely (if ever) acted out aggressively past the first grade.

It is because of cases like Luis's that I have always attempted to provide more behavioral support strategies to preschool teacher teams. I think every preschool team would benefit from identifying the coercive cycle and the importance of sticking to a structured routine. While the little preschoolers can be full of energy, not potty-trained, and tricky to track and keep progress on, they respond the quickest to good curriculum and good (see also: *consistent*) behavior intervention plans. Preschool behavior intervention plans provide pretty rapid returns on your investment of time. The trick is finding the time up front—but no matter what, it is worth it.

Luis's behavior data are below.

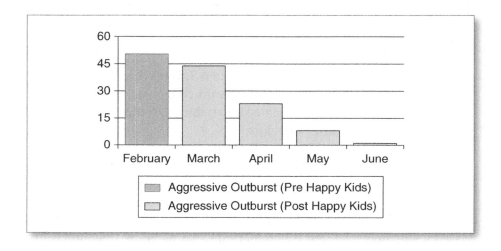

Luis's team monitored aggression in the form of property destruction or physical aggression. He was intense for the months of February and March, and you can see how quickly he responded to the planning and consistency of the structure the team organized.

ANNIE

When I think of Annie, I remember her intense glare, quirky sense of humor, and strong will to get things right. She wasn't exactly a perfectionist, but she certainly strived to do her best in regard to her academic performance. This drive was also present as she shopped for behaviors that would break the will of our team. It was as if her ability to study and learn transferred over to the realm of terrible behavior. She became a student, if you will, in the art of frustrating adults.

The results of Annie's functional assessments indicated that she acted out either (a) to escape unwanted demands and/or activities or (b) to gain the attention of an adult or peer. When it was all said and done, Annie also had an extremely low frustration tolerance. She wanted to do her best in school, and when she was faced with something that challenged or pushed her, she would melt down. Our primary objective with Annie was to teach new, positive replacement behaviors (coping skills) for when she became frustrated.

What I remember most about our intervention with Annie is just how well praise (in large quantities) paid off. We didn't praise her completed work, just her effort. On Annie's desk, we placed two cards. On one card was a visual representation of the negative behaviors we wanted to see decrease (i.e., screaming, hitting, kicking). On another card was a visual representation of the positive behaviors we wanted to see increase (i.e., smiling, positive self-talk, taking breaks). We asked Annie's teacher, Mrs. Slater, to "catch" Annie engaging in the positive replacement behaviors on a timed interval. At first, the interval was set at every 15 minutes, and when that wasn't cutting it, 10, then 5, then 3. While it clearly took some time to get used to, it was remarkable how much increasing the frequency of our praise for her efforts translated into reduced problem behaviors and a huge increase in positive behaviors.

I do remember having an "elephant in the room" discussion with the team about Mrs. Slater's difficulty in adjusting to praising Annie so much in comparison with her other students. This dynamic really bothered Mrs. Slater and understandably so. Mrs. Slater was working overtime for Annie, and the students in her class started to notice. Mrs. Slater possessed a stiff upper lip and was reluctant to let us know how much this bothered her, but we could tell something was up and we asked how we could help. She expressed the frustration, the team listened, and the team came up with a strategy to include a new group of students on the same interval Annie was on. That way, Mrs. Slater was able to praise many students for their efforts, in addition to Annie.

Annie's data are provided below. (Trend lines for good effort went up, aggression trends went down, and taking breaks remained steady throughout the month we worked with Annie.)

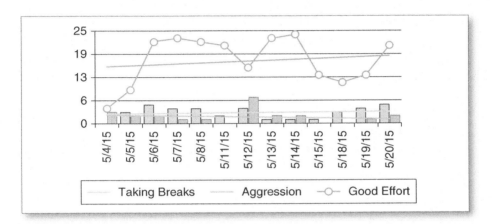

CHRISSIE

Chrissie was pleasant to work with, and I remember her parents being very involved with our efforts. Chrissie was just entering middle school when I met her, and the middle school setting proved much more complicated than I had anticipated. Chrissie's teacher team and counselors worked diligently to support her time spent in the general education setting, outside of her special education classroom. Chrissie enjoyed this process and did quite well in each of her classes. The only time Chrissie seemed to struggle was when unexpected events occurred (like ill-fated changes to the lunch menu). I assume this struggle had something to do with her elevated levels of anxiety and a rigid set of cognitive patterns. For Chrissie, it seemed, there was a very delicate balance among the things in her life. One small change sent the whole house of cards tumbling down.

As curious as her cognitive patterns and preferences were, it was her behavioral outbursts that caused the most alarm and interest in her school. On most days, Chrissie appeared sweet, motivated, and mild-mannered. However, when she became upset—it was scary. I think that was the most notable observation of my time with Chrissie: The contrast between her dispositions was just as difficult to witness as it was to understand.

Our approach (after many hours of observation and consulting with parents, as well as Chrissie) was to take her affinity for schedules, routines, and expectations and make them an asset. We created "Chrissie blueprints" for 3-month periods, where she could review what was going to happen and rehearse those upcoming events in her head (which she did, out loud, daily). We color-coded the blueprints (which were essentially school calendars and bell schedules), specifying areas where unexpected changes had a higher probability of occurring (e.g., homeroom = green, teacher = yellow, lunch menu = red). Any area in the yellow and red, we labeled "uh-oh areas." These areas required "uh-oh plans." Red-coded areas required immediate-attention action plans and crisis tree communications. We had Chrissie help us build her own response to those areas first on her blueprint. Chrissie's preferred uh-oh plan involved visiting a sensory room (a small room adjacent to the special education classroom with a bean bag, swing, and other activities approved by her occupational therapist).

Chrissie's behavior data are provided below.

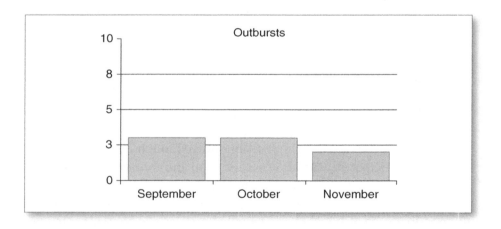

SAMANTHA

Every time I think of Samantha, it brings a smile to my face. I don't know if it was because we both shared an affinity for well-orchestrated profanity and rock 'n' roll *or* because she and her lovely teacher have kept me posted on her progress over the years. (It's probably both.)

There is not much more I can say about Samantha's conditioned response to clapping other than that it simply sent her through the roof. She became so livid, so enraged, that the spectacle almost made you forget how sad it was. She had lived the majority of her life literally programmed to act out aggressively in response to the clapping stimulus.

Her parents were very attentive to this phenomenon early on and had the resources to seek help from multiple experts in the fields of neurology, Applied Behavior Analysis (ABA), meditation, and so on. Despite these efforts, the response continued. Looking back, I think it was just one of those things without a great explanation—an anomaly. I know her exposure to insensitive peers didn't help, and like many of the students with whom I work, Samantha was also navigating the symptoms associated with autism (e.g., difficulty expressing wants and needs, limited social motivation, elevated levels of anxiety, atypical sensory experiences). Looking back, by the time I met Samantha, she had clearly experienced a very stressful young life.

Samantha was 21 years old when I met her and was in the second year of her post–high school program with the school district. Post–high school programs are great opportunities for students with disabilities to transition from their roles in the school setting to more independent and vocational roles appropriate for their age.

Samantha's particular post–high school program was run by an incredible educator named Mrs. Harmer, who worked tirelessly to create meaningful post–high school experiences and opportunities for each of her students. Samantha was preparing to work at Best Buy (in the media/music department) around the time I met her. When Mrs. Harmer and I consulted with Samantha's team and parents, we performed a cursory records review and noticed that since her entry into the post–high school program, there had been a notable drop in frequency of the clapping response behavior. It didn't take us long to conclude that Samantha's exposure to classmates was the biggest change. Mrs. Harmer's program placed Samantha in the community for the majority of her day, with little (if any) direct interaction in the school setting. This was worth celebrating, and we wanted Samantha to know how well she was doing and that this new world outside of school was going to be less stressful.

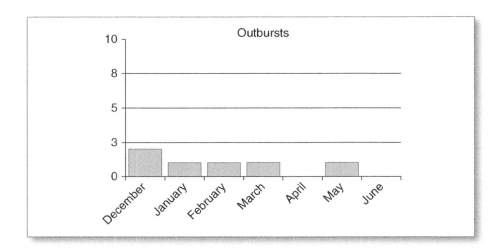

We created the following visual schedule (see Figure 5) to help her conceptualize the risk of clapping. We conjectured that while her conditioned response to clapping was probably not going anywhere, if her outlook and coping skills improved, her stress would be reduced. We hoped that if her stress and anxiety levels were reduced, then perhaps when she was confronted with clapping, her response wouldn't be as intense.

Over time, with help from her team, the visual schedule, and her flow-like challenges at work, Samantha began to acknowledge that she was mostly exposed to "low-risk" areas for clapping. As a result, her comfort level in the community was observed to increase. For instance, aspects of her

Figure 5 Samantha's "Risk of Clapping" Schedule Outside the School Setting

SAMANTHA'S COLOR SCHEDULE

→ High Risk of Clapping

→ Medium Risk of Clapping

→ Low Risk of Clapping

TIME	ACTIVITY	LOCATION	NOTES
7:45-8:00 AM	Morning Jobs/Prep	Transition Program	
8:00-10:00 AM	Exercise	Transition Program	
10:00-11:00 AM	Monday: Meal Plan	Transition Program	
	Tuesday: Library	Transition Program	
	Wednesday: Computer	Transition Program	
	Thursday: Recycle	Transition Program	
	Friday: Meal Plan	Transition Program	
11:00-12:00 PM	Lunch & Hygiene	Transition Program	
12:00-2:00 PM	Monday: Silver Mountain S/J	GYM	
	Tuesday: Silver Mountain P / Holiday Inn	GYM / Hotel	
	Wednesday: New Park / Hampton Inn	Transition Program	
	Thursday: Furburbia / Walmart	Pet Store / Retail Store	
	Friday: Silver Mountain J / New Park	GYM / Hotel	
2:30 PM	Go Home		

personality like joking, smiling, and self-deprecation were revealed to a degree we simply had not seen before. Throughout the following year, there were only two incidences where she lost control, but she rebounded quickly. Her successful interview and placement at Best Buy was a significant moment, and while the stress of holding a paying job was not lost on Samantha, she worked dutifully in her role as an employee. In her tenure at Best Buy, there was never a CD or DVD out of alphabetical order—ever. She could find anything requested of her in the media section. (I'm not sure how many customers ever bothered her for facts about the music and films, but when they did, they were in for a treat. She knew everything they would ever need to know about an album, a track, and the instruments the musicians played.) Samantha was happy, and the longer she spent away from the school setting, the happier she became. Last I heard, Samantha had attended a live concert at the House of Blues in Las Vegas. When the crowd clapped and roared, Samantha simply smiled.

TINO

The time period with Tino was frenetic and stressful but ultimately satisfying. I distinctly remember being very grateful for the support from Tino's parents and the determination and compassion of his team. The faculty and staff with whom I worked suffered serious bite marks and bruises, yet they continued to try to help Tino move past his biting behavior. It was hard not to be impressed by their dedication.

I mostly remember being concerned for Tino. He seemed to experience a significant amount of difficulty processing language, and his ability to regulate his sensory needs was notably impaired. He loved being outdoors and engaging in gross motor activity and spinning, and for a while, we got him to play tag (then he got bored with us).

I remember discovering that practicing the principles of ABA is just that—practice. Enlisting the dynamics of ABA seems to be a constant process of refinement and, well, analysis! When I think back to this time period, I think that was when I became very aware of the importance of antecedent management.

I learned to honor the formula and the steps of the ABC sequence. It was tempting to try to be a hero and draft a series of consequences and punishments for Tino's biting all those breasts. It has been my experience that this "hero mindset" is strong among many practitioners, parents, and administrators. It is as if the only important step in behavior management is the consequence. Skipping steps A and B is silly because we can miss out on identifying new behaviors to teach (e.g., keeping teeth behind the lips) and making basic adjustments like arm's-length proximity, without even having to think about a punishment. It has been my experience that managing the environment and teaching new behaviors is much less difficult than managing consequences. Below is an example of how we collected data targeting behaviors to decrease and behaviors to increase.

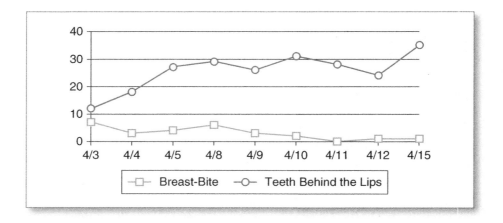

Appendices

Appendix A

The Coercive Cycle and How to Break It!

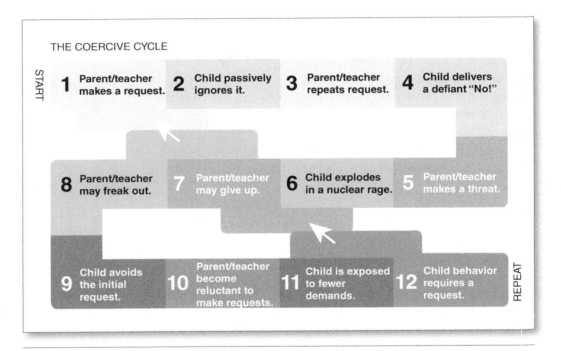

THE COERCIVE CYCLE

| START | 1 Parent/teacher makes a request. | 2 Child passively ignores it. | 3 Parent/teacher repeats request. | 4 Child delivers a defiant "No!" |

8 Parent/teacher may freak out. | 7 Parent/teacher may give up. | 6 Child explodes in a nuclear rage. | 5 Parent/teacher makes a threat.

9 Child avoids the initial request. | 10 Parent/teacher become reluctant to make requests. | 11 Child is exposed to fewer demands. | 12 Child behavior requires a request. | REPEAT

Created using the Venngage Infographic maker, https://venngage.com/

Copyright © 2018 by Corwin. Available for download at **resources.corwin.com/happykids**

BREAKING THE COERCIVE CYCLE

RECOGNIZE THE CYCLE

1. Does the student go from zero to nuclear in seconds?
2. Do you feel angry? Emotional?
3. Do you feel hopeless?
4. Are you focused on "winning" more than teaching a new behavior?

If you said yes to any of these questions, coercion is at play.

MAKE A (PRACTICAL) PLAN

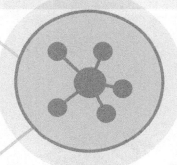

While good plans should always include ABA-based principles like identifying the function(s) of a behavior and teaching a replacement behavior, they SHOULD NOT be overly technical and jargon-y. Our job is to create simple-to-consume-and-execute plans to a team not trained in ABA.

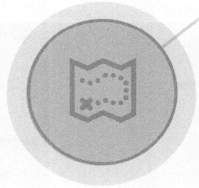

STICK TO THE PLAN

Our ability to remain consistent (not the same as stubborn) with a plan cannot be overstated. Consistency is the KRYPTONITE to the Coercive Cycle. The trick is facilitating consistency across the student's entire team. Measure progress in 2-week chances, pivot, refine, repeat.

Visit www.totempd.com and let us help break the cycle.

Created using the Venngage Infographic maker. https://venngage.com/

Appendix B

RIP Catharsis

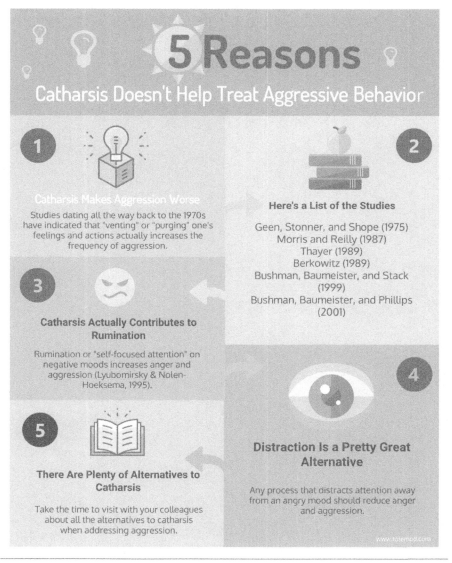

5 Reasons

Catharsis Doesn't Help Treat Aggressive Behavior

1 Catharsis Makes Aggression Worse

Studies dating all the way back to the 1970s have indicated that "venting" or "purging" one's feelings and actions actually increases the frequency of aggression.

2 Here's a List of the Studies

Geen, Stonner, and Shope (1975)
Morris and Reilly (1987)
Thayer (1989)
Berkowitz (1989)
Bushman, Baumeister, and Stack (1999)
Bushman, Baumeister, and Phillips (2001)

3 Catharsis Actually Contributes to Rumination

Rumination or "self-focused attention" on negative moods increases anger and aggression (Lyubomirsky & Nolen-Hoeksema, 1995).

4 Distraction Is a Pretty Great Alternative

Any process that distracts attention away from an angry mood should reduce anger and aggression.

5 There Are Plenty of Alternatives to Catharsis

Take the time to visit with your colleagues about all the alternatives to catharsis when addressing aggression.

www.totempd.com

Created using the Venngage Infographic maker, https://venngage.com/

Appendix C

RIP Corporal Punishment

The Case Against CORPORAL PUNISHMENT

 THE VERDICT IS IN - Corporal punishment contributes to more aggression in children. The American Academy of Pediatrics (1998) concluded that corporal punishment is ineffective at best and harmful at worst.

 THAT'S NOT ALL - Eighty-eight studies conducted over 62 years concluded that 94% of the individual effect sizes of corporal punishment represented undesirable behaviors or experiences (Gershoff, 2002).

 LINKED TO CHILD ABUSE - Meta-analytic studies have confirmed a strong association between corporal punishment and physical abuse. In the United States, approximately 13 of every 1,000 children under the age of 18 have experienced abuse or neglect (U.S. Department of Health & Human Services, 2001).

 SHARE - It is remarkable what an impact popular opinion has on the research in areas such as corporal punishment. Join the safety revolution in our schools and share this document liberally.

www.totempd.com

Created using the Venngage Infographic maker, https://venngage.com/

 Copyright © 2018 by Corwin.
Available for download at **resources.corwin.com/happykids**

Appendix D

The Better Reprimand

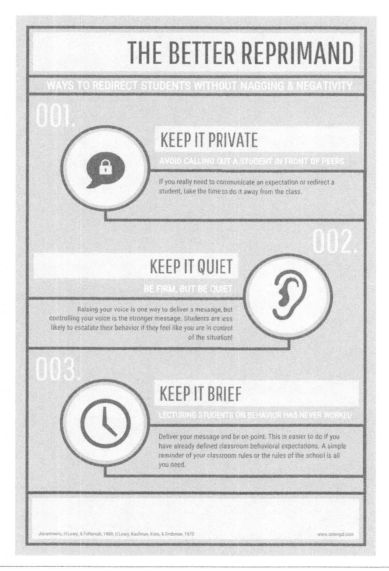

Created using the Venngage Infographic maker, https://venngage.com/

Appendix E

Differential Reinforcement of Incompatible Behavior (DRI)

The DRI Drill: Targeting Replacement Behaviors

Try differential reinforcement of an incompatible behavior (DRI) BEFORE you deliver a reprimand.

Pick a Behavior

If there is a particular behavior a child is struggling with, label it! **For example:** hitting or shouting out.

Then pick a behavior that is incompatible with what you labeled. **For example:** hands to the side or quiet voices.

Find the Incompatible Behavior

Survey your environment. If the child with whom you are working is exhibiting the negative behavior, find another child in proximity that is exhibiting the new, incompatible behavior. **For example:** Target student is not coming in from recess, so you praise all the students who are coming in from recess.

Watch for an Opportunity

While you are reinforcing all the other children for engaging in the incompatible behavior, watch for an opportunity to praise the target student.

Even if the student makes an approximation to your targeted behavior, praise them. Let them know they're close.

 www.totempd.com

---

Created using the Venngage Infographic maker, https://venngage.com/

Appendix F

Identifying Core Beliefs When Considering Discipline

Most behavior interventions for kids miss their mark because they focus on the superficial aspects of behavior.

Real change comes from validating the emotion of the child and understanding where the emotion comes from.

All of us (kids included) hold core beliefs that drive our emotions and our behaviors.

While we must act to prevent aggressive behavior, we must also work with the child to identify what core beliefs are contributing to their behavior.

Self-Esteem
Self-Efficacy
Self-Worth

Created using the Venngage Infographic maker, https://venngage.com/

Appendix G

*List of Evidence-Based
Screening Tools*

5 Evidence-Based

SCREENING TOOLS

1 Systematic Screening for Behavior Disorders (SSBD) from Walker and Severson, 1992

2 Behavioral & Emotional Screening System (BASC-3/BESS) from Kamphaus and Reynolds, 2007

3 Student Risk Screening Scale from Drummond, 1994

4 Strengths and Difficulties Questionnaire from Goodman, 2001

5 Social Skills Improvement System: Performance Screening Guide from Gresham and Elliott, 2008

This list is neither an endorsement nor designed to be comprehensive. It is designed to provide you with a starting point if you and your principal are interested in screening for behavioral difficulties just like you screen for reading difficulties.

The evidence supporting screening systems to prevent problems is incredibly strong. These programs can start you down the path to meaningful student (and teacher) support.

Created using the Venngage Infographic maker, https://venngage.com/

Appendix H

*Steps to Conduct a Basic Pilot
(Feasibility) Study in Your District
to Screen for Behavioral
Problems in Students*

PREWRITTEN OVERVIEW
TO PROVIDE STAKEHOLDERS

Every year, in every school, in every grade, and in every classroom, there is a handful of students with significant emotional and behavioral problems. Not only are these students more likely to struggle academically and socially in school, but their difficulties are more likely to extend beyond the school years into adulthood.

School resources appear to be quite limited in the domain of difficult student behavior. The limitations are, of course, unintentional. They arise for any variety of reasons. Teacher training programs simply do not have room to dedicate to sufficient instruction on effective classroom management. Instead, teachers are asked to learn as they go, and about 50% of all new teachers actually leave the profession due to the lack of support for poor student behavior. School guidance personnel (i.e., school counselors, school psychologists, school social workers) are typically assigned to an entire school, take on multiple responsibilities, and simply do not have enough time in the day to address student needs directly.

These limitations are in contrast to academic approaches in schools. When students are struggling to organize math facts or read passages fluently, they are identified and provided with the appropriate school-based resources to try to remediate their struggles. When students are struggling to organize their behavior and attend to grade-level tasks, they are typically not provided with the appropriate school-based resources because either (a) such resources do not exist or (b) there is no personnel to provide them adequately.

The results are twofold: (1) Students with externalizing behavior problems receive ineffective "reactionary" discipline from administrators, and (2) students with internalizing behavior problems walk through school unidentified, unnoticed, and underserved.

The goal of establishing a "behavioral and emotional student screening protocol" is to create a tiered approach to behavior management within the school system.

Tiered approaches to health, academics, and behavior are all designed to (1) identify problems, (2) provide solutions, (3) prevent serious problems, (4) assess severity of problems, (5) allocate appropriate resources, and (6) ensure the quality and integrity of the institutions providing the services.

Most children in the United States receive health screenings in the form of immunizations and hearing and vision protocols. Currently, public schools are adopting Response to Intervention approaches in academics to screen for learning disabilities in core academic areas.

Behavior screening is simply one more facet of a tiered approach to student success. The whole idea behind screening en masse is to effectively identify concerns before they become serious problems. Significant amounts of time and money are saved through early intervention and providing systematic support for students identified as struggling with significant behavioral and/or emotional problems.

PROCEDURES: FIVE STEPS TO SUCCESS

Behavioral and emotional screening should be held at least biannually. October and January are good months to conduct the screening. By October, it is assumed that most classroom teachers will have a good general idea about student behavior in their class. January screenings allow for any new developments or even new student additions later in the school year.

For the pilot study, the screenings may take place at a faculty meeting or grade-level team meeting. Principals can decide which venue would be the most appropriate. *It is recommended that the pilot study be conducted in no more than two grades at a single school.*

Step 1

Ask teachers to rank order their students in two separate categories: internalizing and externalizing. Definitions of the categories are provided below.

Internalizing behaviors are best described as behavior problems directed inward by the student, withdrawn from the external social environment, that represent problems with self. Internalizing behavior problems usually involve behavioral inhibition (e.g., overly timid, sad) and low self-esteem. Common descriptors include (a) anxious, (b) socially withdrawn, (c) lethargic, and (d) unassertive.

Externalizing behaviors refer to all behavior problems directed outward by the student, toward the external social environment. Externalizing behavior problems usually involve behavioral excesses (i.e., too much behavior) and are considered inappropriate by teachers and other school personnel. Common descriptors include (a) aggressive, (b) defiant, (c) inattentive, and (d) reactive.

Sample rank-order forms are included in this packet.

Step 2

The rank-order forms are collected by a school counselor, and the student names are reviewed. The following checklist is recommended when reviewing the rank-order forms.

Rank-Order Checklist	Yes	No
Is the student on an individualized education plan? (If yes, consider working with special education case manager to devise behavior plan.)		
Is the student on a 504? (If yes, consider working with 504 team to devise behavior-related accommodations.)		
Is the student seeing the school counselor? (If yes, evaluate adequacy of the intervention and availability of the counselor.)		
Is the student an English language learner? (If yes, consider whether or not any language and/or cultural barriers are contributing to the behavior. Intervene accordingly.)		
Is the student receiving outside counseling services? (If yes, facilitate communication with these services and coordinate efforts at school.)		

Rank-Order Checklist (continued)	*Yes*	*No*
Are parents aware of any behavioral problems? (If yes, open communication with parents and begin problem-solving approaches to student behavior.)		
Does the student have a history of disciplinary problems? (If yes, what has been done in the past to correct student behavior? Is it working? Why or why not?)		
Is the student receiving adequate behavior management in class?		

Based on the information garnered from the checklist, determine whether or not the student concerns warrant more attention. If the team decides the student concerns warrant more consideration, move on to Step 3.

Step 3

Conduct a planning meeting. This meeting should be no longer than 25 minutes and should be designed to make the most out of a problem-solving meeting with school teams. The goal of this meeting is to provide (1) evaluation, (2) support, and (3) a plan summary for identified students.

If parents have not been notified at this point, they should be notified of the results of this planning meeting.

Step 4

Behavior intervention data should be continually monitored and reviewed as part of a behavior intervention plan. The students in this step should receive consultation and support from the personnel available and familiar with providing behavioral supports. Consideration of further school-based resources and potential community-based resources may take place.

Step 5

After the attempt to screen, rank order, and respond to the screenings, be sure to compare supports and behavioral support needs between those that used the screener and those that did not. Answer the questions.

SAMPLE RANK-ORDER FORMS

Internalizing Behavior Problems Rank-Order Form (SAMPLE)

Teacher:_____ Grade:_____ Date:_____

Internalizing refers to all behavior problems that are directed inward by the student, withdrawn from the external social environment, that represent problems with self. Internalizing behavior problems usually involve behavioral inhibition (e.g., overly timid, sad) and low self-esteem.

Examples include:

- Having low or restricted activity levels
- Not talking with other children
- Acting timid and/or unassertive
- Avoiding or withdrawing from peers
- Preferring to play alone
- Acting in a fearful manner
- Not participating in games or activities
- Being unresponsive to social initiations

Non-examples include:

- Acting outgoing, social
- Working on assignments
- Listening to the teacher
- Interacting appropriately with peers
- Following directions
- Complying with teacher requests
- Exhibiting appropriate emotional responses

List Internalizers (Student Names)		Rank Order	
	1		Most
	2		
	3		
	4		
	5		Least

INSTRUCTIONS

1. Review the definition of internalizing behavior, and then review a list of all the students in your class.

2. In the first column, enter the names of five students whose characteristic behavior patterns most clearly match the internalizing behavior definition.

3. In the second column, rank order the students listed in the first column from "most" to "least" externalizing behavior problems.

4. Turn in completed form to district behavior specialist.

Externalizing Behavior Problems Rank-Order Form (SAMPLE)

Teacher:_____ Grade:_____ Date:_____

Externalizing refers to all behavior problems that are directed outward by the student, toward the external social environment. Externalizing behavior problems usually involve behavioral excesses (i.e., too much behavior) and are considered inappropriate by teachers and other school personnel.

Examples include:

- Acting aggressive toward objects or persons
- Arguing
- Forcing the submission of others
- Defying the teacher
- Getting out of their seat
- Not complying with teacher instructions or directives
- Having tantrums
- Being hyperactive
- Disturbing others
- Stealing
- Not following teacher- or school-imposed rules

Non-examples include:

- Cooperating, sharing
- Working on assignments
- Listening to the teacher
- Interacting appropriately with peers
- Following directions
- Attending to tasks
- Complying with teacher requests
- Exhibiting appropriate emotional responses

List Externalizers (Student Names)		Rank Order	
	1		Most
	2		
	3		
	4		
	5		Least

INSTRUCTIONS

1. Review the definition of externalizing behavior, and then review a list of all the students in your class.

2. In the first column, enter the names of five students whose characteristic behavior patterns most clearly match the externalizing behavior definition.

3. In the second column, rank order the students listed in the first column from "most" to "least" externalizing behavior problems.

4. Turn in completed form to district behavior specialist.

Appendix I

Influence Tips From Robert Cialdini

INFLUENCE

(Sales and Buy-In Tips From Robert Cialdini)

1 Reciprocity

If you do something nice for someone, they'll do something nice for you. (You know, like return the favor!) Think about your stakeholders. What is something nice you can do for them?

2 Commitment

Attempt to get some sort of commitment from the stakeholders. They don't have to commit to the entire idea, just part of it. Work toward a formal commitment to your goal in tiny (but accountable) mini-commitments!

3 Social Proof

Share articles, social media posts with stakeholders that include imagery and evidence of how other schools are successfully utilizing an initiative similar to yours.

4 Authority

Authority figures wield enormous influence. People will respect and listen to authority figures who have an important message, an effective style, and a platform from which to speak.

5 Liking

You are going to have more influence the more people like you. That's right, good old-fashioned relationships with stakeholders can really impact how initiatives are adopted (or not adopted).

6 Scarcity

We only have a limited time to begin this initiative! Time is running out! This method of influence is particularly effective when attempting pilot studies. It is only available to a small group of educators. Make it something exclusive.

We All Need Help Getting
Things Done! Try the Six
Principles of Influence!

Created using the Venngage Infographic maker, https://venngage.com/

Appendix J

Applications of RICH Theory to IEP Goals and BIP Goals

IEP GOALS

There are really only two critical variables within every individualized education plan (IEP): (1) Is the plan *meaningful*, and (2) is the progress of the plan *measurable*—M&M. As long as IEP teams keep the focus on these two variables, almost everything else will fall into place. While it may seem simple enough, anyone who works in special education can tell you it is anything but. In fact, for many parents, IEPs have a reputation for being pretty awful.

When we take a step back and look at the IEP process, we can see why this may be the case. Most IEP meetings lose sight of their purpose due to cumbersome procedures, jargon-filled legalese, and the Herculean effort of getting all the necessary information from team members in a timely manner. When IEPs lose their way, meetings become confrontational, and very little benefit is achieved on behalf of the student.

When parents and IEP team members are struggling to see eye to eye on what is best for the student, I have found the inclusion of RICH theory brings everything back into perspective by making our efforts more meaningful. On the next page is a table to help IEP teams and parents who may be stuck when it comes to using special education services. The table uses the domains of human happiness and fulfillment from the RICH theory and cross-references them with common areas of difficulty for students eligible for special education. This table is more of an exercise and planning tool for savvy special educators and parents who really want to focus on the M&M of IEPs.

RICH IEP GOAL-PLANNING SAMPLE

	Meaningful?	*Measurable?*
IEP goal in math	How are the math goals helping the student access resources? How are the math goals helping the student in relationships? How are the math goals helping the student become more competent in math? How are the math goals helping the student keep healthy habits?	How will we know progress is being made or not made? How will you present this information graphically?
IEP goal in reading	How are the reading goals helping the student access resources? How are the reading goals helping the student in relationships? How are the reading goals helping the student become more competent in reading comprehension? How are the reading goals helping the student keep healthy habits?	How will we know progress is being made or not made? How will you present this information graphically?
IEP goal in communication	How are the communication goals helping the student access resources? How are the communication goals helping the student in relationships? How are the communication goals helping the student become more competent in interpersonal communication? How are the communication goals helping the student keep healthy habits?	How will we know progress is being made or not made? How will you present this information graphically?
IEP goal in behavior	How are the behavioral goals helping the student access resources? How are the behavioral goals helping the student in relationships? How are the behavioral goals helping the student become more competent in age-appropriate behavior? How are the behavioral goals helping the student keep healthy habits?	How will we know progress is being made or not made? How will you present this information graphically?

While this table is pretty straightforward, I have found it to be a useful tool when IEP meetings lose their focus on the child. At the end of the day, any goal that considers the RICH domains and can be displayed graphically is a high-quality goal in special education.

Appendix K

The Replacement Behavior Race

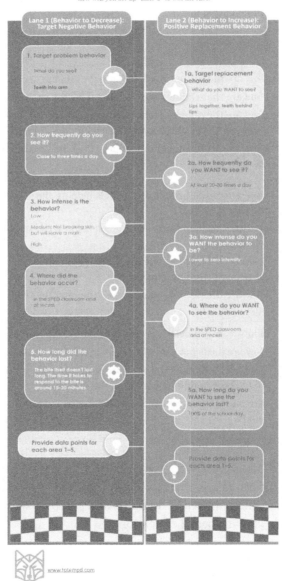

The CORE of your behavior intervention plan will rely on
how well you set up "Lane 2" to win the race.

Lane 1 (Behavior to Decrease): Target Negative Behavior	Lane 2 (Behavior to Increase): Positive Replacement Behavior
1. Target problem behavior — What do you see? Teeth into arm	1a. Target replacement behavior — What do you WANT to see? Lips together, teeth behind lips
2. How frequently do you see it? Close to three times a day	2a. How frequently do you WANT to see it? At least 20–30 times a day
3. How intense is the behavior? Low Medium: Not breaking skin, but will leave a mark High	3a. How intense do you WANT the behavior to be? Lower to zero intensity
4. Where did the behavior occur? In the SPED classroom and at recess	4a. Where do you WANT to see the behavior? In the SPED classroom and at recess
5. How long did the behavior last? The bite itself doesn't last long. The time it takes to respond to the bite is around 15–20 minutes	5a. How long do you WANT to see the behavior last? 100% of the school day
Provide data points for each area 1–5.	Provide data points for each area 1–5.

www.tatempd.com

Created using the Venngage Infographic maker, https://venngage.com/

Initiate your behavior intervention plan here. Use this worksheet to get started.

(Best to include school letterhead on this form.)

(Student) has been observed to exhibit *(target behavior to DECREASE)*. *The behavior may be best described as (information 1). The behavior occurs (information 2), with a (high, medium, low) intensity. The behavior tends to occur in (information 4) and may last up to (information 5).*

In an effort to reduce the (target behavior to DECREASE), (student)'s support team is proposing to teach (student) a positive replacement behavior. For the next 10 school days, the support team will be working on teaching (student) (target behavior to INCREASE). The replacement behavior may be best described as (information 1a). The replacement behavior will occur (information 2a), with a (high, medium, low) intensity. The behavior will occur in (information 4a) and may last up to (information 5a).

Within 10 school days, *(student)*'s support team will evaluate the following areas:

1. How well the support team can identify the target replacement behavior (and reward/reinforce that behavior)

2. The frequency of rewarding the target replacement behavior

3. The intensity of the target replacement behavior (high, medium, low)

4. Where the target replacement behavior will occur (What areas at school/home need to be reinforced the most?)

5. How long the target replacement behavior will last (Make sure the student is clear on what the replacement behavior looks like.)

Appendix L
Reinforcement Checklist

Student Name	Date	Grade	Person Completing Form

Activities (Examples: iPad, swimming, movies, drawing)	Food (Examples: donuts, candy, bagels)	Materials (Examples: stickers, get outta homework free, LEGOs)	Social (Examples: lunch with friends, time with friends, field trip)

Rank Activities	Rank Food	Rank Materials	Rank Social
1	1	1	1
2	2	2	2
3	3	3	3
4	4	4	4
5	5	5	5

Appendix M

Functional Behavioral Assessment Form

Date, Time, and Name of Person Collecting Info	Antecedent (What led up to the event?)	Behavior (Describe exactly what the behavior looked like.)	Consequences (What happened after the event occurred?)

	Escape an unwanted activity/demand	Gain attention of peers and/ or adults	Gain access to a tangible item	Experience sensory stimulation
Provide evidence for the proposed function. Remember, the behavior could have multiple functions.				

Appendix N

*Sample Behavior Intervention
Plan Write-Up*

Your name, credential
Your title
Your ext. 1234
@ your e-mail

mm/dd/yyyy
Behavior Plan for *(Student)*
-Confidential-

REASON FOR REFERRAL

(Use this section to briefly identify student and student concerns. A sample is provided below.)

Currently, *(student)* is qualified for special education services under the classification of *(classification)*. *(Student)*'s parents, faculty, and administration have requested a behavioral addendum to *(his/her)* IEP to help address behavioral concerns. *(Student)*'s behavioral concerns may best be described as:

(Below are sample descriptions of common behavioral concerns. Use them only if they apply.)

  I. Noncompliance

 II. Verbal defiance

III. Physical aggression (e.g., scratching, biting, pinching)

IV. Strange and/or unusual perseveration/preoccupation with staff, schedules, and food

 V. Coercive physical and verbal behavior (i.e., aggression with the intent of getting a specific, desired activity and/or item)

FUNCTIONAL BEHAVIORAL ASSESSMENT

(Functional behavioral assessments (FBAs) can be conducted in many ways. Simply take the time to complete an ABC worksheet. If you've identified an antecedent, defined the behavior, and determined the consequences, you've completed an FBA. A sample of the summary is below.)

A functional behavioral assessment (FBA) was conducted on *(mm/ dd/yyyy)*. The FBA concluded that there *(is/are) (one, two, three, four)* plausible functions of *(student)*'s behaviors. The first function was observed to escape an undesired activity. The second function was observed to gain attention from both peers and teachers.

(Remember, there are only four possible functions of a behavior in an FBA. You will have determined this through your ABC worksheet.)

TARGET BEHAVIORS

(Use this section to define behavioral goals. Use measurable/quantifiable data (i.e., percentages, frequencies, etc.).)

1. 80% compliance to teacher commands (Current compliance at 75% as measured by teacher report)

2. 80% accuracy of using appropriate communication to request attention of peers and/or adults (Current accuracy at 50% as measured by teacher report and classroom observation)

3. Zero physical aggression toward peers, property, and adults (Currently, *[student]* averages 1.5 physical aggression incidents per school month.)

ANTECEDENT CONTROL (ENVIRONMENTAL SUPPORTS)

(A sample of how to complete this section is provided below. (Basically, what are you going to do in the environment to prevent a problem behavior?))

1. Over the past 15 school months, *(student)*'s antecedents or triggering events tended to be related to fluctuations in daily schedules (e.g., late bus, assembly schedules) and the presence or absence of

particular staff members. It is safe to conclude that on days wherein there are few if any schedule changes and consistent staff, *(student)* exhibits very few problem behaviors.

While efforts have been made to minimize the impact of the triggering events, the events cannot be eliminated entirely from *(his/her)* experience in the school setting.

As such, it is recommended that *(student)*'s school team plan accordingly for these events and engage a protocol for days with schedule/staff fluctuations.

The protocol will include the following:

a. Adjusted schedule and activities that limit *(student)*'s distance from trained staff, seat away, and the seclusionary timeout room

b. Inclusion of a physical and visual barrier to vulnerable students (i.e., students confined to wheelchairs, students with limited gross motor/evasive motor skills, students with limited and/or impaired coping/social skills, etc.)

c. Workspace located in close proximity to both "seat away" location as well as seclusionary timeout location

d. Limited plus supervised access to the lunchroom or other less-structured locations throughout the school

2. The protocol will be initiated only on days when there are noted changes in the daily school schedule, as well as noted changes in the presence and/or absence of staff.

3. *(Student)* will continue to have access to the following positive behavior supports:

a. Positive reinforcement system (point system) for targeted positive replacement behaviors

b. Beep tape interval system

c. Highly motivating incentives

d. Posted visual schedule

e. Posted visual rules

f. Ongoing "zone" emotional regulation instruction

4. *(Student)* will continue to have access to typical peers throughout the school day.

CONSEQUENCES

(Use this section to clearly identify what will happen when the target student engages in positive behaviors and negative behaviors.)

When *(student)* provides teachers with adequate-quality assignments and is compliant with teacher requests, *(he/she)* is to be rewarded with points that can earn *(him/her)* access to an incentive of *(his/her)* choice (i.e., free time, no homework, treat, etc.). **At home, swimming or whatever *(he/she)* is interested in.**

When *(student)* engages in fits or episodes of uncontrollable behavior, staff is to firmly provide *(him/her)* with precision requests to calm down and take a "seat away."

If *(student)* refuses to respond to staff precision requests, measures to ensure *(his/her)* safety and the safety of other students must be taken.

For instance, enlist a "room clear" procedure. Teachers should have a code word in place that directs students to leave the area immediately and go directly to a predetermined location (e.g., library). In addition, remove any blunt and/or sharp objects from *(his/her)* immediate vicinity. Enlist *(school district)*'s ASPEN procedures to de-escalate *(student)*'s behavior.

Avoid physical assistance unless *(student)* is in immediate danger of hurting *(him/herself)* or others.

For questions and concerns, please contact *(your name, title)* at *(ext. 1234)*, or e-mail at *(@ your e-mail)*.

Team signatures:

_____	_____
Parent	Date
_____	_____
Parent	Date
_____	_____
Staff	Date
_____	_____
Staff	Date

Staff _____   Date _____

Staff _____   Date _____

Staff _____   Date _____

Staff _____   Date _____

Staff _____   Date _____

Staff _____   Date _____

Appendix O
Behavior Data Infographic

DATA
COLLECTION

Key points and information you should know about collecting data on aggressive/dangerous behaviors

FREQUENCY RECORDING

Simple counting of how many times a target behavior occurs during a designated period of time (e.g., minute, hour, day, week)

FREQUENCY OF BITING BEHAVIOR

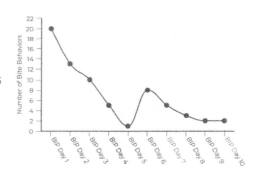

WHAT ELSE?

DURATION DATA

Basic percentage of time that a behavior occurs during the observation

INTERVAL DATA

"Shortcut" for estimating the duration of a behavior. Periodic PREDETERMINED observation periods and records of whether the behavior is occurring.

ANTECEDENT DATA

WHERE and WHEN did the behavior occur? Can you find a pattern? What (if anything) can you modify in the "when" and the "where" to prevent aggression?

YOU MUST MONITOR FOR EFFECTS. DRAW A LINE. . . .

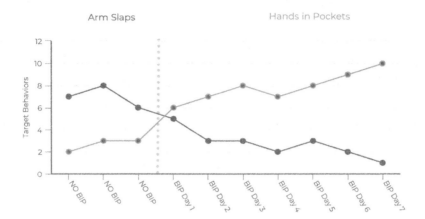

PRE/POST-BEHAVIORAL DATA GIVES THE TEAM A HEADS-UP.

All you need is an x- and a y-axis. Use crayons if you have to! It doesn't need to be complicated or all perfect on a spreadsheet (although, ahem, it's very nice).

Plot progress of target behaviors. Conducting a BIP in ASPEN means you should also be measuring the progress of the new, positive replacement behavior you are attempting to teach.

Establishing a baseline PRIOR to your intervention can be tricky because you don't want any dangerous or aggressive behavior to persist without intervention. In many cases, you may have to ask those affected for an approximate count/duration/frequency of the behavior prior to your intervention.

www.totempd.com

Appendix P
"Hello There, Elephant" Worksheet

The worksheet on the opposite page is primarily a tool for discussion and perhaps reflection. The whole idea is that teams are given the opportunity to openly discuss what may be bothering them about a plan.

HELLO THERE, ELEPHANT!

Most of us know the saying, "Are we going to talk about the elephant in the room?" We use this idiom when there is something bothering somebody and no one is talking about it. When there is an "elephant in the room," things tend to get weird and awkward.

Use this worksheet to preemptively allow team members to discuss their thoughts, feelings, and even reservations about working on the behavior plan.

Thoughts and Feelings About Understanding WHY the Behavior Is Occurring:

On a scale from 1–10 (1 = I don't understand why the student is acting this way to 10 = I totally understand why the student is acting this way) rate your understanding.

1 2 3 4 5 6 7 8 9 10

Thoughts and Feelings About the Drafted Behavior Plan:

On a scale from 1–10 (1 = I don't understand the behavior plan to 10 = I totally understand the behavior plan) rate your understanding.

1 2 3 4 5 6 7 8 9 10

Thoughts and Feelings About Collecting Data for the Behavior Plan:

On a scale from 1–10 (1 = I don't understand how to collect data to 10 = I totally understand how to collect data) rate your understanding.

1 2 3 4 5 6 7 8 9 10

Created using the Venngage Infographic maker, https://venngage.com/

Appendix Q
Thought Replacement Exercises

Rewrite these statements with a more optimistic outlook:

"This is a complete disaster. I can't teach any of my other students."
"Riding the bus is a nightmare. Literally, I have nightmares about riding the bus with her."
"Everything he does annoys me and annoys all my students."
"Why should I spend so much time with this *one* student when the rest of my students are ready to work?"
"Have you met the parents? Yikes. There's nothing we can do."

Appendix R

Emergency Contact Information Form (Template)

If an emergency situation occurs that requires the immediate use of highly intrusive individual interventions to protect the student or others from harm, the staff shall complete and submit the emergency contact information form to the local education agency (LEA) and notify the student's parents within 24 hours.

Student Name	DOB	Grade	School	Staff Members Involved	Date

1. What were the circumstances surrounding the incident (e.g., activity, time of day, location)?

2. Describe the incident/event. (Specifically, what were the antecedent, behavior, and consequences?)

3. Were there any injuries? If yes, please describe in detail below.

4. What could be done to prevent this from happening again?

5. Does the student have a current functional behavioral assessment? Behavior intervention plan?

Staff shall complete and submit the emergency contact information form to the LEA/special education director within 24 hours.

Were the parents contacted? (Circle one):   YES   NO

What time of day were the parents contacted? _____

_____   _____

Signature of person completing form   Date

_____   _____

Signature of LEA   Date

References

Abramowitz, A. J., O'Leary, S. G., & Futtersak, M. W. (1988). The relative impact of long and short reprimands on children's off-task behavior in the classroom. *Behavior Therapy, 19*, 243–247.

Alberto, P. A., & Troutman, A. C. (2012). *Applied behavior analysis for teachers* (9th ed.). Upper Saddle River, NJ: Merrill/Prentice Hall.

American Academy of Pediatrics. (1998). Guidance for effective discipline. *Pediatrics, 101*, 723–728.

Argyris, C. (1960). *Understanding organizational behavior.* Homewood, IL: Dorsey Press.

Baer, D. M. (1985). Applied behavior analysis as a conceptually conservative view of childhood disorders. In R. McMahon & R. D. Peters (Eds.), *Childhood disorders: Behavioral developmental approaches* (pp. 17–35). New York, NY: Brunner/Mazel.

Bain, A., & Macpherson, A. (1990). An examination of the system-wide use of exclusion with disruptive students. *Australia and New Zealand Journal of Developmental Disabilities, 16*, 109–123.

Beck, R., & Fernandez, E. (1998). Cognitive-behavioral therapy in the treatment of anger: A meta-analysis. *Cognitive Therapy and Research, 22*, 63–74.

Bellini, S. (2006). *Building social relationships: A systematic approach to teaching social interaction skills to children and adolescents with autism spectrum disorders and other social difficulties.* Shawnee Mission, KS: Autism Asperger Publishing Company.

Belsey, J., Greenfield, S. M., Candy, D., & Geraint, M. (2010). Systematic review: Impact of constipation on quality of life in adults and children. *Alimentary Pharmacology and Therapeutics, 31*, 938–949.

Bender, H. L., Allen, J. P., McElhaney, K. B., Antonishak, J., Moore, C. M., O'Beirne Kelly, H., & Davis, S. M. (2007). Use of harsh physical discipline and developmental outcomes in adolescence. *Journal of Developmental Psychopathology, 19*(1), 227–242.

Berkowitz, L. (1989). Frustration-aggression hypothesis: Examination and reformulation. *Psychological Bulletin, 106*, 59–73.

Borgwald, K., & Theixos, H. (2013). Bullying the bully: Why zero-tolerance policies get a failing grade. *Social Influence, 8*(2), 149–160.

Bullis, M., Benz, M., Johnson, M., & Hollenbeck, K. (2000). *Effects of job-readiness instruction on special education, at-risk, and typical adolescents.* Unpublished manuscript, University of Oregon, Institute on Violence and Destructive Behavior, Eugene.

Burns, M. K., & Gibbons, K. A. (2008). *Implementing response-to-intervention in elementary and secondary schools.* New York, NY: Routledge.

Bushman, B. J., Baumeister, R. F., & Phillips, C. M. (2001). Do people aggress to improve their mood? Catharsis beliefs, affect regulation opportunity, and aggressive responding. *Journal of Personality and Social Psychology, 81*, 17–32.

Bushman, B. J., Baumeister, R. F., & Stack, A. D. (1999). Catharsis, aggression, and persuasive influence: Self-fulfilling or self-defeating prophecies? *Journal of Personality and Social Psychology, 76*, 367–376.

Carr, E. G., Horner, R. H., Turnbull, A. P., Marquis, J. G., McLaughlin, D. M., McAtee, M. L., Smith, C. E., . . . Doolabh, A. (1999). *Positive behavior support for people with developmental disabilities: A research synthesis.* Washington, DC: American Association on Mental Retardation.

Caspi, A., & Moffit, T. E. (2006). Gene-environment interactions in psychiatry: Joining forces with neuroscience. *Nature Reviews Neuroscience, 7*, 583–590.

Chiaburu, D. S., & Harrison, D. A. (2008). Do peers make the place? Conceptual synthesis and meta-analysis of coworker effects on perceptions, attitudes, OCBs, and performance. *Journal of Applied Psychology, 93*(5), 1082–1103.

Christenfeld, N. J. S., & Leavitt, J. D. (2011). The fluency of spoilers: Why giving away endings improves stories. *Scientific Study of Literature, 3*(1), 93–104.

Cialdini, R. B. (2004). *Influence: The psychology of persuasion.* New York, NY: Collins Business.

Coates, W., Dietrich, J., & Cottington, E. (1989). Trauma and the full moon: A waning theory. *Annals of Emergency Medicine, 18*(7), 763–765.

Cohn. L. B. (1995). *Violent video games: Aggression, arousal, and desensitization in young adolescent boys.* Unpublished doctoral dissertation, University of Southern California, Los Angeles.

Coie, J. D., Dodge, K. A., & Kupersmidt, J. B. (1990). Peer group behavior and social status. In S. A. Asher & J. D. Coie (Eds.), *Peer rejection in childhood* (pp. 17–59). New York, NY: Cambridge University Press.

Cooley, S. (1995). *Suspension/expulsion of regular and special education students in Kansas: A report to the Kansas State Board of Education.* Topeka: Kansas State Board of Education.

Csikszentmihalyi, M. (1991). *Flow: The psychology of optimal experience.* New York, NY: Harper-Collins.

Cullinan, D., Epstein, M., & McLinden, D. (1986). Status and change in state administrative definitions of behavior disorder. *School Psychology Review, 15*, 383–392.

Dabelea, D., Mayer-Davis, E. J., Saydah, S., Giuseppina, I., Linder, B., Divers, J., . . . Merchant, A. T. (2014). Prevalence of Type 1 and Type 2 diabetes among children and adolescents from 2001 to 2009. *Journal of the American Medical Association, 311*(17), 1778–1786.

Diener, E., & Seligman, M. E. P. (2002). Very happy people. *Journal of Psychological Science, 13*(1), 81–84.

DiLalla, L. F. (2002). Behavior genetics of aggression in children: Review and future directions. *Developmental Review, 22*, 593–622.

Drummond, T. (1994). *The Student Risk Screening Scale (SRSS).* Grants Pass, OR: Josephine County Mental Health Program.

Druss, B., & Pincus, H. (2000). Suicidal ideation and suicide attempts in general medical illnesses. *Archives of Internal Medicine, 160*(10), 1522–1526.

Duckworth, A. (2016). *Grit: The power of passion and perseverance.* New York, NY: Simon & Schuster.

DuPaul, G. J., & Stoner, G. (1994). *ADHD in the schools: Assessment and intervention strategies.* New York, NY: Guilford.

Durand, V. M. (2011). *Optimistic parenting: Help and hope for you and your challenging child.* Baltimore, MD: Paul H. Brookes.

Durand, V. M. (2015). Strategies for functional communication training. In F. Brown, J. Anderson, & R. L. De Pry (Eds.), *Individual positive behavior supports: A standards-based guide to practices in school and community-based settings* (pp. 385–396). Baltimore, MD: Paul H. Brookes.

Dweck, C. S. (2008). *Mindset: The new psychology of success.* New York, NY: Ballantine Books.

Edelbrock, C., Rende, R., Plomin, R., & Thompson, L. A. (1995). A twin study of competence and problem behavior in childhood and early adolescence. *Journal of Child Psychology & Psychiatry, 36*(5), 775–785.

Eley, T. C., Lichtenstein, P., & Stevenson, J. (1999). Sex differences in the etiology of aggressive and nonaggressive antisocial behavior: Results from two twin studies. *Journal of Child Development, 70*(1), 155–168.

Elksnin, L. K., & Elksnin, N. (1998). *Assessment and instruction of social skills.* San Diego, CA: Singular.

Fixsen, D., Blase, K., Naoom, S., & Duda, M. (2015). *Implementation drivers: Assessing best practices.* Chapel Hill: Frank Porter Graham Child Development Institute, University of North Carolina.

Fremouw, W. J. (1975). A helper model for behavioral treatment of speech anxiety. *Journal of Consulting and Clinical Psychology, 43*, 652–660.

Gable, S., & La Guardia, J. G. (2007). Positive processes in close relationships across time, partners, and context: A multi-level approach. In A. D. One & M. H. M. van Dulman (Eds.), *Oxford handbook of methods in positive psychology* (pp. 576–590). New York, NY: Oxford University Press.

Geen, R. G., & Quanty, M. B. (1977). The catharsis of aggression: An evaluation of a hypothesis. In L. Berkowitz (Ed.), *Advances in experimental social psychology* (Vol. 10, pp. 1–37). New York, NY: Academic Press.

Geen, R. G., Stonner, D., & Shope, G. L. (1975). The facilitation of aggression by aggression: Evidence against the catharsis hypothesis. *Journal of Personality and Social Psychology, 31*(4), 721–726.

Gerra, G., Zaimovic, A., Avanzini, P., Chittolini, B., Giucastro, G., Caccavari, R., Palladino, M., . . . Brambilla, F. (1997). Neurotransmitter-neuroendocrine responses to experimentally induced aggression in humans: Influence of personality variable. *Psychiatry Research, 66*, 33–43.

Gershoff, E. T. (2002). Corporal punishment by parents and associated child behaviors and experiences: A meta-analytic and theoretical review. *Psychological Bulletin, 128*(4), 539–579.

Giangreco, M. F., Edelman, S. W., Luiselli, T. E., & MacFarland, S. Z. C. (1999). Helping or hovering? Effects of instructional assistant proximity on students with disabilities. *Exceptional Children, 64,* 7–18.

Goodman, R. (1997). The strengths and difficulties questionnaire: A research note. *Journal of Child Psychology and Psychiatry, and Allied Disciplines, 38,* 581–586.

Goodman, R. (2001). Psychometric properties of the strengths and difficulties questionnaire. *Journal of the American Academy of Child and Adolescent Psychiatry, 40*(11), 1337–1345.

Gottman, J. M., & Silver, N. (2000). *The seven principles for making marriage work: A practical guide for the country's foremost relationship expert.* New York, NY: Three Rivers Press.

Gresham, F. M. (1989). Assessment of treatment integrity in school consultation and prereferral intervention. *School Psychology Review, 18,* 37–50.

Gresham, F. M. (1991). Whatever happened to functional analysis in behavioral consultation? *Journal of Educational and Psychological Consultation, 2,* 387–392.

Gresham, F. M. (2004). Current status and future directions for school-based behavioral interventions. *School Psychology Review, 33,* 326–343.

Gresham, F. M., & Elliott, S. N. (2008). *Social Skills Improvement System Rating Scales manual.* Minneapolis, MN: NCS Pearson.

Gresham, F. M., MacMillan, D. L., Beebe-Frankenberger, M. E., & Bocain, K. M. (2000). Treatment integrity in learning disabilities intervention research: Do we really know how treatments are implemented? *Learning Disabilities Research and Practice, 15,* 198–205.

Greydanus, D. E., Pratt, H. D., Spates, C. R., Blake-Dreher, A. E., Greydanus-Gearhart, M. A., & Patel, D. R. (2003). Corporal punishment in schools (Position paper of the Society for Adolescent Medicine). *Journal of Adolescent Health, 32,* 385–393.

Heaviside, S., Rowland, C., Williams, C., & Farris, E. (1998). *Violence and discipline problems in U.S. public schools: 1996–97* (NCES 98-030). Washington, DC: U.S. Department of Education, National Center for Education Statistics.

Hersh, R., & Walker, H. M. (1983). Great expectations: Making schools effective for all students. *Policy Studies Review, 2,* 147–188.

Hester, P. P., Kaiser, A. P., Alpert, C. L., & Whiteman, B. (1996). The generalized effects of training trainers to teach parents to implement milieu teaching. *Journal of Early Intervention, 20,* 30–51.

Hoffmann, S. G. (2011). *An introduction to modern CBT: Psychological solutions to mental health problems.* Oxford, UK: Wiley-Blackwell.

Howard, J. S., Sparkman, C. R., Cohen, H. G., Green, G., & Stanislaw, H. (2005). A comparison of intensive behavior analytic and eclectic treatments for young children with autism. *Research in Developmental Disabilities, 26,* 359–383.

Individuals With Disabilities Education Improvement Act of 2004. 20 U.S.C. 1400 et seq. (2004). (Reauthorization of Individuals With Disabilities Act, 1990).

Jennings, J. R., & Matthews, K. A. (1985). The impatience of youth: Phasic cardiovascular response in Type A and Type B elementary school-aged boys. *Psychosomatic Medicine, 46*, 498–511.

Jenson, W. R., Olympia, D., Farley, M., & Clark, E. (2004). Positive Psychology and externalizing students in a sea of negativity. *Psychology in the Schools, 41*(1), 67–79.

Johnson, S. M., Wahl, G., Martin, S., & Johansson, S. (1973). How deviant is the normal child? A behavioral analysis of the preschool child and his family. In R. D. Rubin, J. P. Brady, & J. D. Henderson (Eds.), *Advances in behavior therapy* (Vol. 4, pp. 37–54). New York, NY: Academic Press.

Judge, T. A., & Piccolo, R. F. (2004). Transformational and transactional leadership: A meta-analytic test of their relative validity. *Journal of Applied Psychology, 89*(5), 755–768.

Kahneman, D. (2002). *Maps of bounded rationality* (prize lecture). The Sveriges Riksbank Prize in Economic Sciences in Memory of Alfred Nobel.

Kamphaus, R., & Reynolds, C. (2007). *BASC-3 behavioral and emotional screening system.* Minneapolis, MN: NCS Pearson.

Kazdin, A. E., & Kendall, P. C. (1998). Current progress and future plans for developing effective treatments: Comments and perspective. *Journal of Clinical Child Psychology, 27*, 217–226.

Kehle, T. J. (1989). *Maximizing the effectiveness of interventions: The RICH model.* Paper presented at the National Association of School Psychologists, Boston, MA.

Kehle, T. J. (1999). *RICH-based interventions.* Invited address at the annual meeting of the American Psychological Association, Boston, MA.

Kehle, T. J., & Barclay, J. R. (1979). Social and behavioral characteristics of mentally handicapped students. *Journal of Research and Development in Education, 12*, 45–56.

Kehle, T. J., & Bray, M. A. (2004). RICH theory: The promotion of happiness. *Psychology in the Schools, 41*, 43–49.

Kehle, T. J., & Bray, M. A. (2005). Reducing the gap between research and practice in school psychology. *Psychology in the Schools, 42*(5), 577–584.

Kehle, T. J., Bray, M. A., Chafouleas, S. M., & McLoughlin, C. S. (2002). Promoting intellectual growth in adulthood. *School Psychology International, 23*, 233–241.

Kehle, T. J., Clark, E., & Jenson, W. R. (1993). The development of testing as applied to school psychology. *Journal of School Psychology, 31*, 143–161.

Kindlon, D. J., Tremblay, R. E., Mezzacappa, E., Earls, F., Laurent, D., & Schaal, B. (1995). Longitudinal patterns of heart rate and fighting behavior in 9- through 12-year-old boys. *Journal of the American Academy of Child & Adolescent Psychiatry, 34*, 371–377.

La Greca, A. M., & Lopez, N. (1998). Social anxiety among adolescents: Linkages with peer relationships and friendships. *Journal of Clinical Child Psychology, 26*, 83–94.

Lahey, B. B., & Loeber, R. (1994). Framework for a developmental model of oppositional defiant disorder and conduct disorder. In D. K. South (Ed.), *Disruptive behavior disorders in childhood* (pp. 139–180). New York, NY: Plenum Press.

Lane, K. L., Kalberg, J. R., Parks, R. J., & Carter, E. W. (2008). Student risk screening scale: Initial evidence for score reliability and validity at the high school level. *Journal of Emotional and Behavioral Disorders, 16*(3), 178–190.

Lane, K. L., Wehby, J., & Robertson, E. J. (2008). How do different types of school students respond to school wide positive behavior support programs? *Journal of Emotional and Behavioral Disorders, 15*, 3–20.

Lanyon, R. (2006). Mental health screening: Utility of the psychological screening inventory. *Psychological Services, 3*, 170–180.

Levinson, H., Price, C., Munden, K., Mandl, H., & Solley, C. (1962). *Men, management, and mental health.* Cambridge, MA: Harvard University Press.

Locke, J. (1690). *Essay concerning human understanding* (Vol. 1). J. W. Yolton (Ed.). London: J. M. Dent & Sons.

Lorber, M. F. (2004). Psychophysiology of aggression, psychopathy, and conduct problems: A meta-analysis. *Psychological Bulletin, 130*, 531–552.

Lyubomirsky, S., & Nolen-Hoeksema, S. (1995). Effects of self-focused rumination on negative thinking and interpersonal problem solving. *Journal of Personality and Social Psychology, 69*, 176–190.

MacMillan, D. L., Gresham, F. M., & Forness, S. R. (1996). Full inclusion: An empirical perspective. *Behavioral Disorders, 21*, 145–159.

Marks, S., Schrader, C., & Levine, M. (1999). Paraprofessional experiences in inclusive settings: Helping, hovering, or holding their own? *Exceptional Children, 65*, 315–328.

Mash, E. J., & Terdal, L. G. (1997). Assessment of child and family disturbance: A behavioral-systems approach. In E. J. Mash & L. G. Terdal (Eds.), *Assessment of childhood disorders* (3rd ed., pp. 3–68). New York, NY: Guilford Press.

Maslow, A. (1968). *Toward a psychology of being* (2nd ed.). New York, NY: Van Nostrand Reinhold.

Mayo Clinic Staff. (2016, November 18). Screen time and children: How to guide your child. *Mayo Clinic.* Retrieved from https://www.mayoclinic.org/healthy-lifestyle/childrens-health/in-depth/screen-time/art-20047952

Miller, W. R., & Rollnick, S. (2002). *Motivational interviewing* (2nd ed.). New York, NY: Guilford Publications.

Miller, W. R., & Rollnick, S. (2004). Talking oneself into change: Motivational interviewing, stages of change, and therapeutic process. *Journal of Cognitive Psychotherapy, 18*, 299–308.

Milton, J. (1667). *Paradise lost and paradise regained.* New York, NY: New American Library.

Morris, W. N., & Reilly, N. P. (1987). Toward the self-regulation of mood: Theory and research. *Motivation and Emotion, 11*, 215–249.

National Association of Colleges and Employers. (2015). *Job outlook 2016.* Bethlehem, PA.

Ogden, C. L., Carroll, M. D., Kit, B. K., & Flegal, K. M. (2014). Prevalence of childhood and adult obesity in the United States, 2011–2012. *Journal of the American Medical Association, 311*(8), 806–814.

O'Leary, K. D., Kaufman, R. E., Kass, R. E., & Drabman, R. S. (1970). The effect of sound and soft reprimands on the behavior of disruptive students. *Exceptional Children, 37*, 145–155.

O'Neill, R. E., Albin, R. W., Storey, K., Horner, R. H., & Sprague, J. R. (2015). *Functional assessment and program development for problem behavior: A practical handbook* (3rd ed.). Stamford, CT: Cengage Learning.

Patterson, G. R. (1976). Parents and teachers as change agents: A social learning approach. In D. Olson (Ed.), *Treating relationships* (pp. 189–215). Lake Mills, IA: Graphic.

Patterson, G. R. (1982). *Coercive family process.* Eugene, OR: Castalia.

Patterson, G. R. (1993). Orderly change in a stable world: The antisocial trait as a chimera. *Journal of Consulting and Clinical Psychology, 61*, 911–919.

Patterson, G. R., Capaldi, D. M., & Bank, L. (1991). An early starter model predicting delinquency. In D. J. Pelper & K. H. Rubin (Eds.), *The development and treatment of childhood aggression* (pp. 139–168). Hillsdale, NJ: Erlbaum.

Patterson, G. R., Dishion, T. J., & Chamberlain, P. (1993). Outcomes and methodological issues relating to treatment of antisocial children. In T. R. Giles (Ed.), *Effective psychotherapy: A handbook of comparative research* (pp. 43–88). New York, NY: Plenum.

Patterson, G. R., Reid, J. B., & Dishion, T. (1992). *Antisocial boys.* Eugene, OR: Castilia.

Pittenger, L. M. (2015). Emotional and social competencies and perceptions of the interpersonal environment of an organization as related to the engagement of IT professionals. *Frontiers in Psychology, 6*, 623.

Quinn, J. F. (2015). The affect of vision and compassion upon the role factors in physician leadership. *Frontiers in Psychology, 6*, 442.

Regalado, M., Sareen, H., Inkelas, M., Wissow, L. S., & Halfon, N. (2004). Parents' discipline of young children: Results from the National Survey of Early Childhood Health. *Pediatrics, 113*(Suppl. 6), 1952–1958.

Reid, J. B., Patterson, G. R., & Snyder, J. (2002). *Antisocial behavior in children and adolescents: A development analysis and model for intervention.* Washington, DC: American Psychological Association.

Robinson, T. R., Smith, S. W., Miller, M. D., & Brownell, M. T. (1999). Cognitive behavior modification of hyperactivity-impulsivity and aggression: A meta-analysis of school-based studies. *Journal of Educational Psychology, 91*(2), 195–203.

Rollnick, S., & Miller, W. R. (1995). What is motivational interviewing? *Journal of Behavior and Cognitive Psychotherapy, 23*, 325–334.

Roose, S. P., Glassman, A. H., & Seidman, S. N. (2001). Relationship between depression and other medical illnesses. *Journal of the American Medical Association, 286*(14), 1687–1690.

Rousseau, D. M. (1989). Psychological and implied contracts in organizations. *Employee Responsibilities and Rights Journal, 2*, 121–139.

Rousseau, D. M. (1995). *Psychological contracts in organizations: Understanding written and unwritten agreements.* Thousand Oaks, CA: Sage.

Russell, B. (1930). *The conquest of happiness.* New York: W. W. Norton.

Sailor, W., Dunlap, G., Sugai, G., & Horner, R. (2009). *Handbook of positive behavior support.* New York, NY: Springer Science + Business Media.

Schein, E. H. (1965). *Organizational psychology.* Englewood Cliffs, NJ: Prentice Hall.

Seligman, M., & Csikszentmihalyi, M. (2000). Positive Psychology: An introduction. *American Psychologist, 55*(1), 5–14.

Shore, L. M., Tetrick. L. E., Taylor, M. S., Coyle Shapiro, J. A.-M., Liden, R. C., Parks, J. M., Morrison, E. W. . . . Van Dyne, L. (2004). The employee organization relationship: A timely concept in a period of transition. In J. J. Martocchio & G. Ferris (Eds.), *Research in personnel and human resource management* (Vol. 23, pp. 291–370). Oxford, UK: Elsevier.

Shores, R. E., Gunter, P. L., & Jack, S. (1993). Classroom management strategies: Are they setting events for coercion? *Behavioral Disorders, 18,* 92–102.

Skiba, R. J. (1999). The dark side of zero tolerance: Can punishment lead to safe schools? *Phi Delta Kappan, 80,* 372–376, 381–382.

Skiba, R. J., Peterson, R. L., & Williams, T. (1997). Office referrals and suspension: Disciplinary intervention in middle schools. *Education and Treatment of Children, 20*(3), 295–315.

Socolar, R. S., Savage, E., & Evans, H. (2007). A longitudinal study of parental discipline of children. *Southern Medical Journal, 100,* 472–474.

Springer, B. J. (2012). *Superheroes in the resource room: A study examining implementation of the superhero social skills program by a resource teacher with students with externalizing behavior problems.* Unpublished doctoral dissertation, University of Utah, Salt Lake City.

Sugai, G., & Horner, R. H. (1999). Discipline and behavioral support: Preferred processes and practices. *Effective School Practices, 17*(4), 10–22.

Sugai, G., & Horner, R. H. (2015). School-wide PBIS: An example of applied behavior analysis implemented at a scale of social importance. *Journal of Behavioral Analysis and Practice, 8,* 80–85.

Sugai, G., Horner, R. H., Dunlap, G., Hieneman, M., Lewis, T. J., Nelson, C. M., Scott, T., . . . Ruef, M. (2000). Applying positive behavior support and functional behavioral assessments in schools. *Journal of Positive Behavior Interventions, 2,* 131–143.

Suldo, S. M., & Huebner, E. S. (2006). Is extremely high life satisfaction during adolescence advantageous? *Social Indicators Research, 78,* 179–203.

Suldo, S. M., & Shaffer, E. J. (2008). Looking beyond psychopathology: The dual-factor model of mental health in youth. *School Psychology Review, 37*(1), 52–68.

Szidon, K., & Franzone, E. (2009). *Task analysis.* Madison, WI: National Professional Development Center on Autism Spectrum Disorders, Waisman Center, University of Wisconsin.

Tantam, D. (2000). Psychological disorder in adolescents and adults with Asperger syndrome. *Autism, 4,* 47–62.

Taylor, S. M., & Tekleab, A. G. (2004). Taking stock of psychological contract research: Assessing progress, addressing troublesome issues, and setting research priorities. In J. A. Coyle-Shapiro, L. M. Shore, S. M. Taylor, &

L. E. Tetrick (Eds.), *The employment relationship: Examining psychological and contextual perspectives* (pp. 253–283). New York, NY: Oxford University Press.

Thaler, R. H., & Sunstein, C. (2008). *Nudge: Improving decisions about health, wealth, and happiness.* New Haven, CT: Yale University Press.

Thayer, R. E. (1989). *The biopsychology of mood and arousal.* New York, NY: Oxford University Press.

Thornton, J. C. (2015). The effect of relationship quality on individual perceptions of social responsibility in the US. *Frontiers in Psychology, 6,* 781.

Tiesman, H., Konda, S., Hendricks, S., Mercer, D., & Amandus, H. (2014). Workplace violence among Pennsylvania education workers: Differences among occupations. *Journal of Safety Research, 44,* 65–71.

Tilly, D. (2003, December 5). *How many tiers are needed for successful prevention and early intervention? Heartland area education agency's evolution from four to three tiers.* Paper presented at the National Research Center on Learning Disabilities RTI Symposium, Kansas City, MO.

Tuvblad, C., & Baker, L. A. (2011). Human aggression across the lifespan: Genetic propensities and environmental moderates. In R. Huber, P. Brennan, & D. Bannasch (Eds.), *Advances in genetics: Aggression* (Vol. 75, pp. 171–214). Boston, MA: Elsevier Press.

U.S. Department of Education. (2012). *Restraint and seclusion: Resource document.* Washington, DC: Author.

U.S. Department of Health and Human Services. (2001). *Child maltreatment 1999: Reports from the states to the national child abuse and neglect data system.* Washington, DC: U.S. Government Printing Office. Retrieved November 28, 2017, from https://www.acf.hhs.gov/sites/default/files/cb/cm99.pdf

Van Acker, R. (2007). *Strategies for dealing with classroom aggression.* Paper presented at the Working Forum of the Council for Children with Behavioral Disorders, Las Vegas, NV.

Walker, H. M., & Severson, H. (1992). *Systematic screening for behavior disorders: User's guide and technical manual.* Longmont, CO: Sopris West.

Welsh, M., Park, R. D., Widaman, K., & O'Neil, R. (2001). Linkages between children's social and academic competence: A longitudinal analysis. *Journal of School Psychology, 39,* 463–481.

Wolf, M. M. (1978). Social validity: The case for subjective measurement or how applied behavior analysis is finding its heart. *Journal of Applied Behavior Analysis, 11,* 203–214.

Wolfe, D. A., Fairbank, J. A., Kelly, J. A., & Bradlyn, A. S. (1983). Child abusive parents' physiological responses to stressful and non-stressful behavior in children. *Behavioral Assessment, 5,* 363–371.

Zargar, M., Khaji, A., Kaviani, A., Karbakhsh, M., Yunesian, M., & Abdollahi, M. (2004). The full moon and admission to emergency rooms. *Indian Journal of Medical Sciences, 58,* 191–195.

Index

Page numbers followed by f indicate figure
Page numbers followed by t indicate table

A SAGE Publishing Company

CORWIN HAS ONE MISSION: to enhance education through intentional professional learning.

We build long-term relationships with our authors, educators, clients, and associations who partner with us to develop and continuously improve the best evidence-based practices that establish and support lifelong learning.

Solutions you want. Experts you trust. Results you need.

Author Consulting

Author Consulting

On-site professional learning with sustainable results! Let us help you design a professional learning plan to meet the unique needs of your school or district. www.corwin.com/pd

Institutes

Institutes

Corwin Institutes provide collaborative learning experiences that equip your team with tools and action plans ready for immediate implementation. www.corwin.com/institutes

eCourses

eCourses

Practical, flexible online professional learning designed to let you go at your own pace. www.corwin.com/ecourses

Read2Earn

Read2Earn

Did you know you can earn graduate credit for reading this book? Find out how: www.corwin.com/read2earn

Contact an account manager at (800) 831-6640 or visit **www.corwin.com** for more information.

Made in the USA
Coppell, TX
19 May 2023